Debra,

Enjoy the journey through the pages and know that Love is . . .

NOW and Forevermore

Thankyou for being a part of the birth of this book With Love
Denice Fecketter
1/25/04
NWN ☺

Denice Fecketter

Cover Photo by the Author
First Dawn of the Millennium
Poverty Bay, New Zealand
1/1/2000

Published by Higher Shelf Publishing,
an imprint of Pronghorn Press

HIGHER
SHELF
PUBLISHING

a t
www.pronghornpress.org

Dedicated through the
Love of generations
to our daughters
Carolyn and Cheryl
and their loved ones.

Introduction

It began in the most conventional way. On Saturday morning September 16, 2000 I began to type my story on a Handheld PC after I heard a suggestion for a beginning from a TV show on the art of writing:

"I'm only here for one reason: to tell the story..."

I chose to begin my story by referring to my husband, Raymond, who had died twenty-three years earlier. It's not unusual to begin a story with a traumatic event, but the inner voice prompting me said that it was my husband's Spirit, Raymian, who would write the story with me!

As I took up the project I experienced many feelings about what we were doing. You will see within these pages my doubts, questioning and growth as the work comes to fruition. (My words and thoughts are set in italics for simplicity.)

This co-created book is filled with both comfort and revelation. It explores why we are all here and what our challenges are. It encourages the understanding that all those we have loved are with us and pleased to communicate with us any time we are willing to accept their guidance.

I hope that you will find something here that reassures you, touches your heart, expands possibilities, and brings Light to your search and Love to your Life.

Denice

Part One

The Agreement

Now it is time
to fulfill the promise
you and I made
before our life together,
to bring Love to the world
through these writings.

9/16/00 *at home*

My husband, Raymond, who died almost twenty-three years ago, has come back to me.

Let me explain. He wants me to work with him so that "we might complete what we set out to do before entering into the lifetime we shared. Our 'work' will be to bind words into letters covering subjects which are not explored in the ordinary course of conversation. The questions asked will not have answers in the ordinary sense."

His request that we work together comes as a surprise to me. I know that life is not over at death. And although Ray communicated with me in dreams for many years, I did not expect him to return as an inner voice that would guide what I write.

Now, he comes again as the Spirit Raymian:

Our hearts are bound together in common calling to a new way of life that crosses the dimensions. We have previously agreed to work together as one, to carry the word forth so that all may know of this possibility of communicating between the dimensions. It is a gift, a possibility. Our hearts will know the way.

I must follow my own heart. I have struggled with the notion that if I *do what he asks, I would seem to be forsaking the flesh for the Spirit. Even though it seems weird, I have decided that "nothing ventured is nothing gained." I am enamored of the possibility of having fun, being joyous in this new type of a relationship. I look on this as creating possibilities that will enhance my life and my Spirit, now and forevermore. I know that this can end at anytime; therefore, I am willing to begin.*

Raymian, what say you?

I am pleased that we will continue to work together, as we have known that we will be together forevermore. We are of One, so how else can it be? Our Soul-hearts are drawn from the same Source. Our hearts tell us that we know what is right for us. So we begin again.

I did not know this was the path when I was on Earth, in form. I felt very comfortable knowing you, and you me. We seemed to communicate without openly communicating through words, but rather knowing. This is a little different. Here we are communicating also without words. But you and I must use words for the purpose of sharing our communication with all who want to share our relationship.

This is a new experience of being in two levels of reality at the same time. I speak and you hear within, not without. You record what I say, as well as your thoughts, hopes and dreams. Meanwhile, our Love is the tie that binds our two worlds together.

We are the communicators. We are the entities. We are the lovers of life alive on Earth and in the hereafter. Our hearts are full to overflowing with Loving energy. It melds in the thought patterns that produce this missive.

Take this as our first Love letter from us, on this side of the veil, to your world of Light Beings. We are Light and Love. Now all shall know that we exist in this form and shall begin to alter their way of communicating to a way based on this knowledge. We are here to spread the "word" that all who live on Earth share the heavens and all that abounds above and below.

So be it.

I love you. I am with you always.

Raymian

Our Love
is the tie
that binds our two worlds
together.

9/29/00 at home

I am here with you at all times. We will pretend that this is a communication that has a beginning and an end. That is so only in a linear world, one with Time and distance, one with rules and regulations that form our means of communication. It is so that we can record our thoughts, and not let them meander throughout our conscious being. We will be disciplined in the way of communication; though this framework limits us.

There is no boundary to our communicating. It is prevalent day and night, night and day, always, in the night or day or in places where there is no night or day. Communication is available on all levels and in all dimensions all at the same time. We have to filter that which we want to pay attention to.

We choose to hear what is said, to feel what is felt, to Love that *is*.

We are all spiritual beings and we are coming to a new way of *Be*-ing. It is obvious that it shall be limitless, or shall I say, "without bounds?" Our hope is for Love to be the means of communication from me to you, from you to me. We are One; therefore, our communication is known to each of us as if it originated within one.

What can you tell me about my upcoming trip to India?

It will be an enlightening experience. By that I mean, while there you shall be immersed in the shelter of one's Love in such a way that you will know of what we speak.

Our hearts are our Sources of Love. That is, we enter into the knowing through the portal of our heart. That is difficult to understand for those who only "think." Instead, it is for us to communicate with each other through the heart-means.

Many of your teachers on Earth are beginning to notice that there is more than one way to communicate. It is for them a means that appears to be little used. You know that the heart is the way, the portal. It is the way of ease in communication, for it is the Truth that is communicated, not the superficial trappings of the mind. Of course, mind and heart work together. They beam forth the Light of Knowing and the Love of *Be*-ing. Together we shall *be* in a new way that is not limited by the makings of the mind.

Raymian, can we continue with our love letters?

I am here to be with you in this endeavor. Our hearts are joined together as we proceed. We say that it is Love that permeates all. Actually it is Love which is *All That Is*. A force as strong as Love can leave no doubt about our knowing that it is the Love that abides within us which is responsible for our hearts' energy.

We find our Truth in the heart of things. That is true of all things, of *All That Is*. Truth is the force of Love. No other force is as powerful. *Seem* to be with one another, and you shall not be there. *Be One* and you shall be. That is the force of these words, a harbinger of things to come.

We have experienced the love of life. It is true togetherness in the life force. We know each other from the moment we are born on

Earth. We recognize our forcefulness when we encounter each other's form. It is recognition of the internal knowing that speaks to us.

When I first saw you, we were playing at the bowling alley: a joke, a bet, and then payment of the wager. We bet on each other: that we would recognize our Souls as we prepared for life together. Our spirits were high. Who won the bet? We both did, for it was the entrance to a new way of life for us.

That night at dinner, I remember how you struggled to pronounce my last name. You had to write F E C K E T T E R on the napkin. I know of no one else who had such a hard time saying it. I also know that you sometimes feel that it is a moniker that belongs to someone else. And yet, you have borne the name of Fecketter longer than any other. Enough said about our first "date."

How can we live with one another and feel as if someone else is living our lives?

It is because we disassociate from our everyday experiences. To take another's name disassociates us from our original family. Taking a new name is meant to begin another family, not to forget the other. Our name does not say who we *are*. It is temporary, for that name, too, shall be laid aside, perhaps on our gravestone — though it will rest in the hearts of those who knew us in this form.

Our lives on Earth are temporary forms of who we are. We *are* the Light and the Love that shines through our destiny. We have more to be and to do once we pass over. Our destinies are joined in both worlds. It is a way of Earth's future: to know the world of vision, and at the same time communicate with invisible dimensions.

I have been waiting for this day since I left the Earth form. It was sudden and unexpected. Here one minute and gone the next. How I wished that we had time to say goodbye! But only the love I felt for you could pass through the dimensions. I felt as if the world had ended. And indeed, the world we knew together was afterwards to be lived by you alone.

I went on to learn more in the new dimension, but I never forgot you, nor did I leave you for very long. The trauma of leaving so quickly was difficult for me. I wished that I could have answered the phone that night when our neighbor, who was raising money for an annual flower sale, called to ask me to buy a dozen roses for you. But I was already gone, too soon.

Raymian

Our lives
on Earth
are temporary forms
of who we Are.

9/30/00 *at home*

I am with you today as we are together always. Our hearts have joined in this way to be one for all to see. Our hopes and dreams are the Life/Love of *All That Is*.

Our hearts are transparent. We can see deep within each one's Soul. That is an experience of Love making it easier to communicate with one thought growing out of combined energies. Our Soul is the Soul of all who herald the way of the worldview to come. We are open, transparent, all-seeing and all-knowing. Nothing is hidden.

Every thing is visible when seen through discerning eyes. By that I mean, we cannot see all that is as a jumble of things, experiences, and thoughts. We can only know that which we *choose* out of all there is. This limiting focus shall continue, yet we proceed to attempt to bridge the gap between what is now known and what is to be accessed in the future.

Our love did not die when I left. Well-meaning individuals told you to put aside my memory so that you could proceed. That is good advice if you are looking at opening yourself to a new way of *Be*-ing in the life that you have yet to live. But I was not advised to do the same on this side.

I was bound to your Spirit by our commitment we made before entering the Earth plane. Thus I was to continue our relationship in a new way: watching over you and our daughters, as well as my mother and other members of my Earthly family. You and I had also proposed to keep in touch. First it was done by me hovering in your dreams.

There were occasional visitations as our daughters were honored for their work at school. I was there, and you knew it, for you felt my presence comforting you. I went away for awhile, for we have much to do here, in this life. Now, it is time to fulfill the promise you and I made before our life together, to bring Love to the world through these writings.

I understand more about relationships. We come and go, meeting one another, and then moving on. Sometimes we have a fleeting glimpse of true connection. But, alas, it is gone in a flash. I have struggled with understanding what it means to encounter another person. My shift from permanence and long-term relationships is to the realization that all worldly relationships are impermanent, that is, only temporary in the Earthly sense.

I detect sadness in you that no relationship seems to be long term. That is only so if you look only at the Earth beings. "Here today and gone tomorrow," that is the mantra of today's living. But this missive spells out a different story: A willingness to continue a relationship begun in one dimension into, through and beyond that dimension — a relationship that connects the two dimensions at the same time. This is a novel approach for you and I seek not to continue what we had, but to build anew with energies we know and trust.

Raymian

Our love
did not die
when I left.

10/3/00 on the train to NYC

Raymian, I enter the new ground of loving through the dimensions.

It is not easy to know one another this way, for we have history between us that was accumulated in the Earth dimension. Our Love surpasses all understanding of one lifetime together. Instead, it holds onto past understanding in new ways.

We were comfortable in our Earth ways. It was almost uncanny how we knew what each other's reactions would be. We had a relationship that was characterized by freedom to think and do without the poison of possessiveness.

You went your way and I went mine until that last Friday night. That was when I stayed too long away from home. I wondered whether you would care, as I thought to call you. But I was not sure if my phone call to tell you I would be delayed would matter. Deep down inside, I thought it would. I thought I should call, but I didn't because we had an agreement that we each could go our separate ways without having to ask permission. But somehow I knew that this night was different. I had never stayed away that long without letting you know where I was. When I finally came home, I was greeted with "never do that again."

It was the first and only ultimatum. I then knew you cared

deeply about my welfare and me. I knew that I would never hesitate to call if I decided to stay out long after the normal time to appear. Then, only four days later, I did not appear for dinner on time. It was too late, for I had passed over at 5:20 P.M. while making arrangements for my school's faculty holiday party.

So ended our time together.

Raymian

You should know how worried I was the night you stayed to talk. Never before had I worried because I had an inner sense that everything was all right. That Friday I expected you earlier. I had a sense that something was not normal. So we both knew that things should have been done differently. Now I know that it was a necessary foreshadowing of times to come. Just four days later you kept your promise to "never do that again."

I grieved. I held the hope of your return. It was not to be so in the way that I imagined.

10/04/00 *at home*

Raymian, do you have a letter for me?

I communicate in many ways. It is Love personified. My Love is with you always. You feel fatigued because you are entering a new way of *Be*-ing. It is not that you will die to this world, but you will leave behind that which you have accumulated, that which you have carried with you as a burden. Blow the cobwebs out of your mind! Clear out the corners and cupboards that have stored the memories of past ways! We need not carry with us all that was, only all that is. This is a special way of viewing the world through a lens unencumbered by past ways. It is Joyous lightness to be without all of that past!

You ask how letting go of the past is related to us, you and I. We shared much in life but now we carry forth only our Loving energy that we can apply to our current existences. We know that the Joy is with us to use in whatever way we see fit. Our Love is felt as Joy, free and clear, pure and flowing. No more capturing the moments and storing them away to relive. We only continue through our existence, forevermore. Our hearts *are* Love.

So be it.

Raymian

*Clear out
the corners and cupboards
that have stored
the memories of past ways!*

10/9/00 at home on Columbus Day

Our hearts are joined beyond the way of Love-giving in the normal sense of the word. By that I mean, we have come to know our ways are of this Earth *and* beyond. Our hearts source the Love, giving us a new sense of well-being. It is our gift to the world as we pass through.

Our hopes are transparent, too. We love each other, only to be separated at death. That is not the way it is meant to be. Our Souls fill the void with Loving-kindness. We are a part of *All That Is*. We do not disappear. We, on this side, are always here, always around you in Spirit.

Our calmness is an indicator of the peace of Love. It is not generally exciting, but rather *knowing*, kindly flowing from one to another. And yet, it knows no bounds. It is there to be One with *All That Is*.

Our hopes are to continue to focus Love through each other's Spirit. That is, we display Joy to all who tune into the glory of life and Love. We need each other as symbols of Love being incarnate. That is, we exist with and without body or form. It is so good to be with you again in consciousness. That is what I was aiming for: to know you again in existence, but to also across the dimensions. You see, we are always caring. We cannot help but care for the welfare of each other. Our hearts are full of Love and life-giving Light that permeates *All That Is*.

Your thoughts are guarded as we approach a new way of

communicating. We resolve that this is temporary, and only such that it will serve a purpose in this lifetime. It is easy to sway to the other side but we may count on our egos to pull us back to the way of being in which we are currently involved.

I am a gardener. I love to grow plants and people. That is the purpose of this communication, to grow beyond the boundries which we have placed around ourselves. Our focus in this work together shall be planting hope and life renewing attitudes in the path of the derelict hopes that downtrodden persons bear. It is being "without understanding" that produces the despair of those who live without hope of what is to come. Dreams manifest as we proceed. No one need feel the mantle of loss of hope.

Prayer and thanksgiving precede the opening of the Light bearing way. That is the path that we shall illuminate. It is a new way of *Be*-ing, devoid of the darkness that exists in the hearts of many. Are you ready to travel this way? I am.

Raymian

"I am," I say with tight-lipped determination, for I do not know what lies ahead. It is a dubious honor to have chosen this way. I have some misgivings, but as I've said before, "Nothing ventured, nothing gained!"

Now, let us begin this new way of *Be*-ing. It is hope that permeates our relationship. Put that aside, and just *be* with it so that we may proceed without expectations. It is expectation that leads to Joy, but also disappointment. This is not the end result we anticipate.

Instead we are on a journey to explore relationships in new ways. We had a relationship in Earth form. And now, our relationship is with *and* without form. That is so that we can communicate mentally, spiritually and in an all-knowing way. Our hearts are the guides to this new relationship, even though we shall *think* about it, as well as experience emotions. Our aim is to be free, to be One with *All That Is*, and in so doing, to be One with each other.

The other day you said, "I am one who *is*." That is a statement fraught with knowing that you are as you *are*. I am, as I *am*. So that makes us One with our Selves.

So be it.

It is *choice* that governs all that we do. No matter what we do, we *choose* to do it. No one else has chosen it for us for we are co-choosers of our destinies. We can choose a different way at any time. But overall, we shall *choose* that which is right and perfect for us. That is the way.

Our hopes and dreams are harbingers of that which we shall manifest. We know that whatever we *choose*, it shall be that which we have chosen.

So what does this have to do with our relationship?

It is only clarification of the fact that we have each *chosen* this path, this way. Each of us has *chosen*; therefore, we shall continue on our way.

It is a way that is brightened by our long-standing recognition that Love binds us together. There may be times when we seek confirmation, but that is only for others' benefit, for the readers' edification. There are some true-life examples that will be shared from time to time, but do not come to depend upon those episodes.

We are talking about a new way of *Be*-ing which does not need examples from the past. It is not dependent on the past for we are here *now*. That is all. What we share is not stories of past relationships, but an example of Love that passes through the ages to those who are open to *knowing* in their own way. Our hearts are bound with Love-giving forces that can encounter *All That Is*. Is that not what is important, both to you and to me?

You hold too tightly to the past. After twenty-three Earth years all that *was* has dimmed. Let that be. And now, let us proceed to the new day. Our hearts are open.

We each have lessons to learn as we proceed. We will grow through those learnings. Our lesson today is to *be in the Light*. That is, to nurture the flame that grows within the being. It is fueled by Love, our Love for each other and the Love of *All That Is*. We nurture our Spirits with Light sources that are in us *and* beyond us.

The sun shines with warmth. The Earth gives forth its Loving energies. The light of the sun is transformed on Earth to plants and animals that feed each other, that nurture each other, in turn. We are gifted with our lives and the lives of all others. We have an opportunity each day to share and nurture others, as well as be nurtured by them. It can be one big Love feast, each increasing the beauty and force of one another.

Instead, we tend to focus on the individual. That is good for growing strong, but what else is there? To be alone in this world is no fun. We can enjoy our own company, but what is better than joining forces with another and feeling the force of that synergy? We can choose to combine our energies for so much more.

Our hopes and dreams can be magnified when shared with one another. Try it and see that together we can be synergy, feeling the warmth and Joy of Love personified at a higher level than one can accomplish alone. *Share* the Joy. *Be* the Joy. It is the Love of *Be*-ing in synergy with *All That Is*. That is why we do this writing together: to know the Joy of co-creating. We are not alone. We are together, now, and forevermore.

So be it.

Armand

Why did you sign off "Armand"?

Because I *am* Armand. The Love that you feel is mine. Do you remember that I liked to be called "Ramón"? It is of the same Light of Love. I have many aspects to explore. One of these is Raymian.

We are of the same Source. So I guide you as teacher and as husband. We have shared many lives together, as we have played many roles. I came to you first as Armand, the harbinger of Love to come. I come to you as a figment of your imagination, as I tell you stories that you repeat. We are *all*; therefore, we come in many aspects.

You can distinguish between our energies, but that is actually indistinguishable from all beings. We fool you not. We blend sometimes. I shall be more careful to maintain the distinction for the time being. C'est la vie.

I feel like I'm being played with by entities from beyond. I do not want to be less than a full partner in this relationship. I want to know who is speaking so I can relate appropriately. That is all.

You can get your dander up! Your objection is well taken. If we are to co-create then you shall know at all times who is speaking.

Armand

Is Raymian the Soul with whom I spent sixteen years?

Yes.

What is his relationship to Armand, the guiding Spirit?

It is he, in form. We are all One; therefore, we can communicate the Soul part that you knew on Earth. Our other "Selves" are part of the greater whole, *All That Is.*

You are currently Denice. It is a part of the higher Spirit that continues to be without form. Your greater Spirit is ours, too; therefore, we are Oneness. We can communicate in personal Spirit. That is to say, we form personifications that can talk with one and other. It is this Spiritual Being that we identify with.

We are moving to greater spiritual communications so that we all may know that all the world is One. You may choose one personification over another. But for the purposes of this dialog, the Spirit shall be in the name of Raymian, who spent time with you, who shared your life with you. He is someone you know and trust. That's what makes this message special: to know that the Spirit lives on and can be contacted even after the body dies.

Seek not complete understanding in this way. Trust that you shall record all that is through Raymian.

So be it.

Raymian

That's what
makes this message special:
to know
that the Spirit lives on
and can be contacted,
even after the body dies.

10/11/00 at home

I am here in Spirit. Our Love is what ties us together. It is that we know who we are which makes a difference to us. We please ourselves as we go about our daily ways. We have goals to accomplish. It is the fruit of those ambitions that we cherish.

I know another way: to *Be* in the moment so fully that I am consumed, totally. That is, I meld with Time, Spirit, Love, and become One with *All That Is*. It is at that moment that I know the Truth: that higher ambitions cannot take me to higher heights. There is but one way of *Be*-ing: to be truly Love, Love of the moment, and Love of *All That Is*. Can you imagine any greater *Be*-ing than to *be* Oneness personified? Only those who have experienced this Oneness can know the Joy of which I speak.

We have much to do to bring understanding of Love and Light to this world. We each do this in our own way. But some of us have committed to Loving in such a way that the world can experience through our sharing of our experience.

Perhaps you can recall a moment when we felt Oneness. Do you remember how we shared the birth of our children? We did not know that their Spirits would be born out of a moment of our complete Oneness, sharing ourselves with each other in such a way as to produce another born out of ecstasy. So our Love grows, not only within our hearts but also in the hearts of our daughters. They, too, have passed their Love on to their husbands, and together to their children. We seldom think of passing Love on from one generation to the next, but it is so.

Melding and building families of Love begotten.

Our Source is Love. Our Light shines forth with that Love. Our touch conveys Love. Our eyes see Love. And our hand extends that Love, offering it to strangers touched by the moment we share. How little we understand of the passing on of Love, not only from one generation to another, but also from one person to another.

We need not come face to face with another person to convey Love for Love permeates *All That Is*. It is present when we are present. It is shared knowingly, as well as unknowingly. A smile says it all. We *are* Love conveyed through that smile or glance or by just being present. We make a difference wherever we are. Our absence is felt when we withdraw, though we can travel on thought to destinations around the world. "I send you my love," is a statement filled with Love that travels from one place to another, from one person to another. Continue in Loving ways and your destiny shall be fulfilled.

And now in the name of Love I bid you adieu.

Raymian

To hear
our heart's desire
is the lesson
of today's world.

10/19/00 at *Pizzeria*

Our hearts are open to many experiences. We have our hopes and dreams of Love fulfilled. Ours, yours and mine, is a dream, continuing throughout lifetimes. We have been together for many millennia. Time counts not in the way of *Be*-ing. It ticks off the moments but they are not consecutive. We please ourselves by testing the times. It is a game to play: "here today and gone tomorrow." Of course tomorrow never comes, for we are in the moment only.

Our hearts expand to that which is beyond the moment in our thoughts. But in reality, there is no *beyond*, for we are all here *now*. It is a concept which we must study to accept; for we have been trained to think in a certain way, to understand what we can convey to others. That is a false supposition, for we are, as we *are*, now and forever. Our hearts tell us that this is so.

Our hearts tell us many things, but we have been trained to not listen with our hearts. To hear our hearts' desire is the lesson of today's world. We must recognize that our hearts have something to say. We *know* that is so, but we have closed down our portals to the heart's memory. We have ignored what we *know* in favor of what others think we should know.

Now is the time to *know* our Selves, heart and Soul. It is for us a journey of faith. We *know* some things deep down inside. We must trust what we *know*. Our hearts are opening to this new way of *Be*-ing. It is for us a journey to the heart of matter. That is the way to the center of our beings.

So be it.

Our hearts, yours and mine, are blended. By that I mean, that we Love each other at the core of our beings. We have been parted for twenty-three years on Earth. That is so that we each can grow independently without the intrusion of each other's forces.

Our hearts are bound together. That is, they are Oneness. To be separate is a misnomer. And yet we are together and apart at the same time. Our hearts are bound but our psyches are separated by the veil of Time.

It is a way of *Be*-ing in several dimensions at one time. We can each access the other by stilling ourselves and asking for the other to appear in our hearts. Focus brings us together, though we are always there, willing to be there for the other. Your focus today: the anniversary of my leaving. There is no regret today, only Joy of knowing that all can be together again in this life and beyond. Our hearts tell us to sing the songs of Love's lasting beyond all separation. It is so.

So be it.

I come to you with Love in my heart. It has been difficult to sustain that Love over the years. It fades in the light of many daily tasks, and just doing. But I know now that Love is my heart's Source. I needed to open the chambers closed so tight by grief. There was no one to love in the same way, as I knew with you. I shut out the possibility because I thought that I was too physically weak to share my energy with another.

Little did I know that holding the Love unexpressed drained my physical body. To hold back that which should be expressed is a destructive act, one that destroys the holder's own Self. To free myself of the need to constrict my feelings is a gift to my Self and to the world of "others." I no longer hold back. I find that expression and freedom to expand feeds my Soul and those of others surrounding me.

I am thankful that I lived long enough to learn this lesson, even though the road was a lonely one. I now know that I was never alone. I just thought I was. Now I know you are always here with me, night and day. It is comforting, but at the same time not restraining, for I know that our relationship supports me. It does not prevent me from forming new relationships on Earth. As a matter of fact, I believe it will encourage new relationships.

That is so. Our love is not at this time a physical love. It is a Love of all beings. It is founded in the heart's chamber — its Source — the Love of *Be*-ing.

We can continue to *be*. That is what we did not understand when I was an Earthling. Our Souls are immortal, lasting through the eons. We now *know* that this is so.

Our hearts are again open. Whatever passed between us is now openly shown to be a blip in Time for we have an everlasting bond that will go on and on. Together we will continue to experience the Love of each other.

So be it.

Raymian

Our hearts' desire
is to find the core
of our Selves.
It is within.

10/21/00 at home

I am of one mind for I have but one heart and Soul. By this I mean, that we are thinking with One mind, as well as knowing what is to come. Our hearts' desire is expressed through our caring for one another. It is telling us that our lives are lived through our minds' eyes. That is, we *see* without seeing. We *know* without knowing. We *come to this place* without being here.

It is unlikely that we realize what we are doing for we come to this place not knowing our force is bound within us. We seek ourselves *outside* ourselves. We look to others for our validation. It is so telling to seek and find that which is not there, for we are *within*, not without.

Our esteem is Soul-centered *not* "other"-centered. It wells up from *within*. We must know our Selves to be One with *All That Is*, not separate entities who must be fed from without. Our hearts' desire is to find the core of our Selves. It is *within*.

So be it.

Raymian

10/21/00   *evening at home*

Our hearts are opening to *All That Is* within us. It is for us to find a way to open ourselves to the Source of *All That Is*.

So be it.

I am with you. You are one who is seeking a way to tell tales that will convey the Truth. It is our commitment that we shall tell these tales together. Remember that we are communicating between dimensions. That is a tale in itself!

Many people communicate this way unknowingly. By that I mean, they think that it is their imagination to hear a departed Soul talk with them. It is natural to communicate cross dimensions. But many people have been taught that this is not possible. I implore those who espouse these ideas to try it. At first they may think it is their imagination but eventually they will come to trust this type of communication.

Raymian

At first
they may think
it is their imagination
but eventually
they will come to trust
this type of communication.

10/22/00 outside Pizzeria

Our hearts are open as we begin this communication. Our Love permeates all that we do. It is a foolish notion that we *are* what we *do* for we *are* One. That is all. For this explanation I shall convey the Truth through a story:

The story begins with a lover seeking a mate. The lover does not know who this might be in the beginning of the search. They encounter many others, but seek only one. When one is seeking, it is surface characteristics that one first perceives. That is the way we present ourselves to the world. But it is not these surface characteristics that we seek. It is that which permeates all that we *are*. It is the Love connection!

Many vibrations are permeating our atmosphere. From all of these we will select the ones that resonate closely to our fundamental vibration rate. It is compatibility in Love, the energy force that we exude. It is easy for us to notice this compatibility if we are open to such a thing. For it is meant to be a complementary force that completes our way of *Be*-ing in the world. Together, we have the strength to proceed. It is sometimes said that "two are better than one." The Truth is that Oneness surpasses all else.

So be it.

I have been waiting to say that Love is eternal. That is, it lasts not only a lifetime, but *forever*. It is difficult to understand such a statement when one thinks there is an ending to the story of a lifetime. But it is so that we can experience Love personified in many forms. To exist in only one form is to limit our experience. We have the capacity to render ourselves anew throughout the ages. It is so that we may experience what it is to be *without* the eternal Love Source.

Of course that is not possible for our hearts are forever replete with the elixir of Love. But we have the ability to shut down the Source, as if it does not exist. That is the way that we have lived our many lives thus far, as if Love does not exist.

It is difficult to explain something that one has not experienced, it is as if it doesn't exist. We can talk about Loving or *Be*-ing, but until one actually experiences what we are talking about, they have nothing to relate to.

Sometimes we have had a glimpse of that which I speak. That is because Love is all around us, as well as within us. Our armor is not so complete that a little Love can't be felt, from time to time.

We expect the Love we are seeking to come from others. Therefore, we seek it in others, only to be disappointed because love from a source outside ourselves cannot be sustained. Love grows *within* us. We merely allow it to flow. What we mustn't do is shut the Love down. We can confine it within its Source. We can even reverse the flow.

The flow of Love is expansion. When we constrict our hearts' own Love by fearing *that which is to come,* we stop the outward flow. We hesitate, and the flow is constricted. Any act which constricts Love or draws it back unto our selves, is an act of withholding the Love force.

As this energy builds within us, it causes a damming of the flow. From time to time that dam may burst forth with pent up energy, destroying that which is in its path, instead of nurturing all that is nearby. Our hearts are meant to be open, unconstricted. When we close down to protect ourselves, we destroy ourselves from within.

I remember that we played with the children. As we did that, our hearts opened with the most beautiful expressive Love. Their hearts were open, too. We fed each other's Love.

It is a shame that as adults we teach children by withdrawing Love. We break the spirit of those who come to us as our children when we criticize all that they do. It is meant for us to nourish each other with open hearts, not that we punish the spirit that explores. We find ourselves sooner by nurturing the spirit of all those with whom we come in contact.

So be it.

I know that you want me to refer more to our time together. It is unlikely that I will do so consistently for we are on a new path that is one of growth of *Be*-ing. Be not disappointed that we shall continue in this way.

Our hearts are open to new ways of *Be*-ing. We are creating this new way of *Be*-ing together. We shall move forth in Love and Light, now and forevermore.

Raymian

When we close down
to protect ourselves,
we destroy ourselves
from within.

10/20/00 at home

Dear Raymian,

I would like to continue with our love letters.

I am enamored by the potential of our writing. It is for me revealing a connection to loved ones beyond "normal" reality. We know that this form of communication is distinct from that which we normally engage in. Our hearts are open when we communicate in this way. It also means that we have re-learned to listen with our hearts, as well as speak with our hearts.

So much that is said on Earth is couched in conventionalities. By that I mean, we hide our true feelings behind our remarks. We think about the impression we will make if we say such and so. That is, what we speak is not true to ourselves or to others. We do not always speak the Truth. We weigh what we say against that "impression" that is so dear to us.

We teach our children to lie when their words might hurt someone else.

We cover our Selves with a facade that becomes what the world sees. It is not *who* or *what* we *are*. It is the shell we have built around ourselves, word by word. Cracking that shell is the first step. We have grown so encrusted with un-reality that we cannot tell the barnacles from the flesh. Our hearts are covered with a shell so thick that we think it is impenetrable. When someone says, "Open your heart," we know not what he or she means.

We hear, "Love permeates all! That is the way: to Love one another." But what is this *Love*? It permeates all, and yet we cannot get a hold on it. It appears elusive to the person seeking Love. It appears always to be somewhere else. "If only I could grab hold of it! Drink from the fountain of love. Suck up the love that others send toward me!" It is elusive to the person who feels devoid of Love. Their search is an external one. And as that person encounters the Love flowing forth from others that he or she will vacuum up that Love, leaving its source drained. We all know people who suck the energy from others, leaving them depleted. That is not the way to the Source of Love.

Look *within*. Seek the heart of the matter. We are all beings possessed of divine loving centers. We have the Source *within* us, though for some of us, it is encrusted with time's residue, piled year upon year upon our heart centers.

Again, we seek a way through this debris hardened around our hearts. You *know* that Love permeates *all*. That is so. It matters not what the substance of the matter is, be it as hard as a rock or strong as steel, it matters not. For Love passes through *all* barriers, be they material or merely misconception.

Our hearts are opened by Love. That is the way to melt the wall built around the heart. We start with one act of kindness, a smile shared with others. It takes little acts of Love to begin the process. Only one who experiences Love can expand upon it. We do not need to absorb the Love of others beyond the limits of their energies. We *share* Love. Love expands outward from all of its sources. It nourishes us. We, in turn, nourish others. It is an expansion of life forces contributing that which we all *are*, to each other and all that is around us.

We have spent too much time on Earth mired in self-pity. That is the way to squander Love. To focus the force of Love on one's own sadness absorbs the Light of Love into the darkness. Here it cannot be utilized for it is held within the psyche, destroying free flowing Loving energy, preventing it from being used in Loving acts. That is the secret of dissolving pain. To allow Love free flow is to dissipate the painful and to re-create in the world.

And now, I bid you adieu, for Love is flowing again throughout the world.

So be it.

Raymian

Who says that the heart
is always open?

Indeed it is not.

10/25/00 at home

I look forward to recording our letter tonight. I have been searching for the right words to tell you what is in my heart. It holds many memories of which I am quite fond. It is for us a way to tell tales that might benefit others and ourselves. I know that Love dwells within our hearts.

It is true that we express this Love in many ways. Be it through a smile, an act or kindness or just *Be*-ing with one another. Who says that the heart is always open? Indeed it is not. We find that hurtful words can cause us to shut ourselves down.

We find that only Joy can sustain an open heart. It is our aim to find a way to express Joy, to experience Joy through all that we *are*. Joy is the expression of Love, night and day. It is the essence of Love expressed through the psyche. We find Joyousness in our hearts. The Love and Joy wells up and fills us, brimming forth. "We are Love," we say. We can *feel* Love. We can express Love as Joy fulfilled. Our hearts know that of which I speak.

Love is a Joyous expression of that force that rises within us. When it is shared with others, warmth flows forth. Others detect the energy flow. Sometimes this is at a subconscious level. Other times we just know that we have felt the force of Love. We are bathed in its brightness and feel Joy within our Souls as we encounter our Love flowing forth from within us, as well as from those around us. We cannot help but know that "Love is in the air," so to say.

Our hearts are opened as we experience the Joy of Love. Remember the love of natural beauty that filled our hearts as we watched the sun rise over Buttermilk Falls? A sense of closeness to the Earth and a wonder of the dawning of a new day filled us with Light that permeated our hearts. Together we sat there at the edge of the stream, watching the light grow brighter. Feeling something stir within our Souls as we held onto each other and shared the morning sunrise.

Each day we can relive the wonder of the rising sun. Each day we can experience the rising of the Light, both within us and without. To see the sunrise is a new experience relived. Remember the light comes again and darkness fades. That is so with Love. It rises within us as the new day dawns. Every day is a new day, for our Spirits are renewed as we witness the dawning of a new Light both within us and without.

So be it, now and forevermore.

Raymian

We have the capacity
to hold onto
an idea
that we dreamed up
and
to make it happen.

Later that day

Our hopes are our dreams. We project our desires in a different form of reality that we call dreams. It is confusing to dream and have dreams of a new reality. Our hopes are buds that flower later. We plant the seed in our dream world and bring it to fruition in this world. What we are doing is creating the future world of our dreams.

We have the capacity to hold onto an idea that we dreamed up and to make it happen. Think about the many times you have participated in this practice. It's as if you magically conjured up your future world. It is so. We create our future state by the thoughts and ideas that we project. We can use this practice anytime that we want something. *Think, act* and *manifest.*

We are powerful human beings. We have capabilities beyond that which we have imagined. We rose to this level by exercising the powers of Love and might. We know that Love is the most powerful tool. *Be-*ing in Love is centering our Selves in the state of Love fulfilled. Be not alone in your pursuit of Love-giving forces for we *are* all Love. Let us experience this Oneness fully together.

My Love is renewed as we transcribe our words for they will tell the tale of the dawning of a new day in each and every lifetime.

So be it.

Raymian

Communicating openly between the dimensions shall become commonplace.

10/29/00 at home
changing back to Standard time

"Our hearts are brimming forth" is a new way to describe our Love flowing over the confines of the heart. That is, our hearts are pictured as solid in our minds. The Truth is that there are no boundaries confining the heart, other than the ones that are in our minds. We seek Love as if it had a single Source. It does and it doesn't. Since we are *all* Love, we are *all* Source. It is recognizing that we are part of this greater Love that so many of us struggle with. We *are* Love. We source Love from our hearts' Soul. It, in turn, is part of the greater Source. So we are all part of Oneness. Our channel to the Source is through our hearts, but once there, we discover we are *All That Is*.

So be it.

Today is a leap to another dimension. It is for us a changing, not only of clock-time but also of our attitude toward eternal Time. To keep track of time is useful in daily activities. But to think that Time is the only way of *Be*-ing is a misconception. We are moving from a time-centered way of *Be*-ing to one that transcends Time, as we know it. Our hearts are open to rediscovering our greater reality, one that is unencumbered by Time.

It is also useful to track time for historic purposes that we can share with others. This gives us a reference point that we all share. We can record our experiences, as well as our growth. Indeed, we can "look back" on our ignorance related to this new way of *Be*-ing.

Communicating openly between the dimensions shall become commonplace. We now use it when we "get in trouble" and are seeking help from the divine. It is in the form of prayer asking God, Saints or some beloved departed one to help us. It comes, sometimes, out of desperation. Our prayers are answered and we go on until the next time we feel that we need divine intervention.

I am here to say that one need not get to the point of desperation before communicating with us. We are here to assist you at anytime. That is, we seek the ongoing relationship of friends who discuss and discover together. We are not alone in our desire to communicate. It is Love that is forcing us to be with each other in this way for we know that there are many aspects of each other that are shared throughout lifetimes. This is just another way to share.

It is comforting to know that we are beyond knowing one another only in one way. You seem to be wondering why this aspect did not come to fruition in our lifetime together. We decided to hold this part back, to be experienced as we are now doing. There was enough in our short relationship that bound us together. We had time for the family. And, as well, it was not the time to disclose these aspects to the world.

Much has happened in the ensuing years that have made it possible to disclose this communication. You wrote what you heard for many years, but did not share those writings, for it was not the time. The world was not ready for the ordinary person to say that she communicated beyond the realm of this reality. It was a secret shared only with those who also understood and sought to perfect this type of communication.

Our hearts are filled with gratitude for the struggles that you have engaged in for there were many years when it was difficult for you to "go it alone." We are sure that it was a necessary prelude to the work that we are doing today. For you it was only through questioning and seeking answers from non-ordinary sources that brought you to this point.

The world's view is changing. It will be easier for those who follow to more quickly accept what we have to say. You were one of the earlier waves that will soon reach the shore, only to find many coming behind you.

We saw new ideas permeate our culture in the last quarter of the 20th century. We all knew that change was in the air. We have moved from being told what to do, to a place where we take more personal responsibility for what happens.

Our creative juices are being unleashed, that is, allowed to flow after years of regimentation. Many find that at first they do not know how to act when someone says, "be creative." For all the world stymied creativity as it strove to increase productivity without question.

It was a hard world to live in because so much of it didn't make sense deep down inside. We conformed in our daily work. But that was not so in much of our marriage. You used to ask, "Who says so?" when I would mention something we should do. We actually got into the habit of questioning conventionality whenever we decided to do something!

It was clear that there was more than one way to do something, and if there was, we were going to do it our way. "Our way" was a decision based on what made sense to us, even though we knew no one else who did it that way. Years later, we found that other people were also beginning to do things that we had done for a long time. They had questioned the status quo, read it in a book or heard some new advice on TV.

In a way we were actually pacesetters, ahead of our times, demonstrating a *new* way. To be ahead of the times is not easy. Many people criticized what we did because it wasn't the "right way," the way that they thought was best. It will be much the same with this writing. To some it will come welcomed; to others it will be wrong and unbelievable. Eventually, it will be accepted as an ordinary way to function, enriched by contact with another dimension.

I have enjoyed our morning together. Have a good day, and remember that *All That Is* is One.

Raymian

The world's view
is changing.
It will be easier
for those who follow
to more quickly accept
what we have to say.

Later in the morning

I, too, enjoyed our communication this morning. I am wondering whether I should add my words to this love letter, for we were bound by conventionalities that have now changed. Being in the midst of convention and knowing that it just didn't make sense or feel right was made more comfortable by your willingness to also question what should be. We managed to make our own choices about the ways we conducted our affairs (behaved). You know that I was reluctant to just do things "the way they had always been done." It was because I did not value decisions made by others that did not really fit today's situation. It appeared to me that no harm would be done if we chose our own way. In fact we liked our way of life.

We felt it was important for our children to develop confidence in their own abilities, as well as to have as many experiences as possible without regard to gender stereotypes. This was important to me. I remember our conversation about the fact that we had two daughters. In the beginning you believed that girls could not do things with you that you would have done with a son.

I had been brought up in a family where boys and girls were treated the same. We all had to do the dishes and shared chores regardless of gender. My mother was the only girl with four brothers. She had to stay home and help around the house while her brothers were free to go out to play or later date. My mother felt that there was an injustice and swore that she would bring up her children with boys and girls treated alike. So I came from an unconventional gender upbringing. I was always more interested in the things that boys did than what girls were supposed to do or "allowed" to do. I knew that girls could do the same things that boys could do if convention were laid aside.

When I shared my experience with you I saw you let go of old stereotypical behavior. It was O.K. to take the girls hunting or whatever you had previously thought girls couldn't or shouldn't do. Our girls learned to be comfortable fishing, playing ball, handling tools, etc. They were preparing for the world of today where everyone can try anything without the gender block. We were ahead of the times. Our children did not have to relearn their ways when the culture as a whole began to shift.

In our own way we cut the ties that bound us to convention. We did not try as a family to live up to anybody else's expectations. We knew what was right for us and we did it.

So be it.

Raymian

To be whole
is
to know
one's Self fully.

10/31/00 at Chinese restaurant

Is Raymian there?

Yes, I am Denice. We loved each other in our own way. It was for us a blending of energies as this is, today. By "blending of energies," I mean that we knew each other without having to think about it. We *knew* that we were together.

I remember the night you came to the basketball game that I played in. I was surprised to see you for we had left the invitation open and you came! I knew then that we had something special between us. For you to attend an event such as this was a sign of caring for my interests and for me.

What followed was a deep relationship culminating in Love for *all*. I did not know so many things, which you exposed me to. My life was rather narrow before we expanded together. I knew that you would be one to lead the way, to show me many ways of *Be*-ing.

I did not know that you were afraid to love fully. It is something that we have all learned. It is not a way to be, for we have no control over the fullness of Love. We are mistaken as to what Love is. It is not the romantic notion that permeates our mind and body. Instead, it is Love that exists within the being, allowed to *be* and to expand throughout the worlds.

We cannot control its growth but we do sometimes shut down so that the Love cannot flow. We have a tendency to see lack of Love more clearly than the constant flow of life-giving forces. It is strange that we close off that which is God-given, our birthright, and seek its existence elsewhere. We certainly miss a lot of Love "feelings" that way! Our hearts are open to the Joy that brims forth as we naturally share each other's Love.

Our hearts are full of Love. It is meant to be that way. Instead, we share thoughts of lack of love. How can that be so? It is our way to find something that has been missing. We believe that we need another to complete our energy. It is not completion that we seek, but rather wholeness that is indisputable. To be whole, we merely look within for the answers, for we will find *All That Is* there where we find our hearts' channel of Love. To be whole is to know one's Self fully. It is not to join with another seeking completion.

When two whole beings encounter one another, there is nothing more splendid than the Love forces that they share. We do not need one another, but we do expand the possibilities when we join together. That is the way it was with us. We magnified our potential, whether we were aware of it or not. We now know that living in the same home complements the energies and builds upon them.

Our hearts are opening to new ways of *Be*-ing. It is for us an expression of two Spirits joined as one.

So be it.

We will continue in this way, now and forevermore.

Raymian

For all of us,
the Light
is dawning anew.

11/2/00 on the train from NYC to home

I am here to tell you that Love is divinely bestowed on *all* who are One. That is the lesson for today: that we Love each other with all our hearts and minds.

So be it.

"It is strange to bestow a blessing on all," you say, for we are coming to a point of Love-giving in our everyday life. For all of us, the Light is dawning anew. We fear not for our Selves for we know that we are sacred. By that I mean, that we are *Be*-ing One in life, as well as in the heavens. That is, we come to tell each other of life immortal. Not in the flesh, but in the Spirit.

It is our delight to fasten the door open to the hearts of all creatures. Our motive is to weld the Light of the torch with that which it touches. We know that metal heated to high temperatures will blend through melting its core. It is the same with Love. It wells up to a point where *All That Is* becomes One, indistinguishable from the original parts bound together. So it is that we join our hearts in Love that cools into a new mass, one that is indistinguishable from that where it began.

For each of us the story is different, for we come to this conclusion by many ways. It is so that we can join our heart Lights again in the Light of all newness renewed, forevermore. Our hearts are full. That is the way to gloriousness.

So be it.

Who was that?

I am Raymian. It is for you to know that I represent many ways of thinking. Our hearts are torn sometimes. We must mend our way to the center of Love and Light.

Our greeting is for you to know that many wish to enter the Earth realm. You shall choose who enters through your portal. That is important for you have a purpose that can go unfulfilled if you get sidetracked. A most fitting reference for one who is currently on a train!

May we proceed to the love letter?

Dear Raymian,

I have listened intently to your pronouncements. It is good for me to share my thoughts, too. For if we are to write this missive together, much must come from my heart. I am not used to letting anyone know how I feel. I am coming to a point where it is time that I say what has been on my mind for if I don't, it shall never be recorded for others to share.

Our hearts are bound. I can feel it. I can also feel a sense of remorse for all the things that might have been said these many years. It is as if I have been confined mostly to my own thoughts unshared at the emotional level. I have learned to discard my feelings as signals of inner turmoil. Yet, I know that some of those things that I obsessed about are better left alone. It is the deep feelings unexpressed that I feel the need to commit to record. It is just because some of them have never even been shared with myself.

We say that
we agree
with past judgments
every time
we make another one
based upon
the past.

11/5/00 at home

I am overflowing with tidings of a new way to be. It is as if I am one who is crawling along a gangplank with trepidation, knowing that the end is near, the end of a way of life that has sustained me these many years. I look forward to what will come next but at the same time wonder what will be left behind, for I know that we traverse a world which is impermanent. At every bend, what has come was indeed a learning experience. Even if I felt put upon, it resulted in my own growth. Sometimes what changed was my attitude.

We have been taught that situations are good or bad. That is not so. Each situation stands on its own. It is only our *interpretation* of it that labels it "good" or "bad." For example we say, "Its a good day," when the sun is shining and the temperature is "just right." We label the day. We judge the day based on our preconceived ideas. The day is not good or bad. It just *is*.

Our notions of good and bad come from our past experiences and that which someone has taught us. We know that this is so, based on comparisons that are stored in our memories. We say that we agree with past judgments every time we make another one based upon the past. That is a vicious cycle going round and round with our opinions and actions based on the past and our present judgments.

Our climate is determined by the moisture in the air circulating around the Earth. Sometimes it obscures our view of the sun. But the sun continues to shine whether we can see it or not.

Precipitation determines our moods. When it rains it pours forth-new life, but we see only the dullness of the day that keeps us from playing. This is a time for renewal. We should not feel that a little rain must impede our progress. It only shows us another way to be on those days when the sun is hidden by the clouds. So it is with our hearts. They are closed on rainy days, out of habit.

It is time to look at our ways of behaving when we think the sun is not shining. For all is there. It is our perception that clouds our knowing and affects our attitude. We know deep down inside that the sun is always shining. We may not be able to see it, but it is there within our hearts, as well as beyond the clouds.

Our hearts are open to new ways of *Be*-ing. It is our hope to be that which we *are*, now and forevermore.

So be it.

Raymian

We have been taught
that situations
are good or bad...
It is only
our interpretation of it
that labels it...

11/5/00   at home in the evening

Why do I feel that I must express subdued feelings?

Only those who are crying out feel the need to be other than what they are. It is for you an opportunity to say that you are healed. Your feelings are cleansed.

That is so. Our hearts are open. Our minds are clear.

So be it.

Raymian

11/6/00

Raymian,

What is there to say that has not already been said? Only that I loved you for those many years. We had a relationship that was comfortable. Now I feel detached, not crying out for a continuance. Too many years have passed.

Like many things on Earth, love fades when it is not nourished. The girls do not remember either. From time to time they might talk about something we did, but for the most part memories have faded. This is not to say that we are not thankful for the relationship. We are. And we have gone on to form new relationships that build upon our experiences together. But they are new relationships that stand-alone. They are not tied to past relationships.

I am usually happy to see someone with whom I had a bond in the past. But often the other person does not share the Joy of reuniting. To them it was a passing relationship that has passed. It does not require more than a nod of recognition. There are no ties that bind them to that relationship.

Our relationship is past. It is made up of memories once lived. I could feel the emotional ties to the past as we mentioned certain episodes. But now I would like to explore the future relationships with our many aspects.

At first I didn't want to stray from the voice of Raymian. As a matter of fact I sort of chastised you for coming from a different aspect when I was tied to Raymian. I am ready now to proceed.

Part Two

Communicating Love

Our hearts are open to developing
our communication skills
in a way
not previously thought possible.

11/13/00 at home

So let us begin anew. Our hearts are open to a new way of *Be*-ing. It is for us a continuous re-examining of past experiences mixed with the new. We come from experience. That is, we learn to remember that which we have experienced. If we did not remember, everything would always be new and the context would be different. So it is for us.

We hold onto our memories of past relationships but are willing to proceed from here with a new relationship. So it is as people change in life. The father who no longer remembers his child, no longer shares memories of times past. He only knows the *moment*, as Alzheimer's has cast away his memory.

If we lived only *in* the moment it would be devoid of the past, too. It would be difficult for us to appreciate what we have if we had no comparison. Therefore, we are bound to our experience in this linear world.

But what if we could engage in a new way of *Be*-ing that melds life's experience with the boundless knowledge of the Universe? Would we not expand our experience to include more than one world at a time? We could tap into the "unknown" as easily as the known without having to change form to do it. The richness of *knowing* combined with the matter-of-fact way of living would surely enhance our experiences.

You ask, "Why now?" It is because we are ready to meld the worldview into something far greater than that which is confined to Earth. We have often supposed what might lie beyond this limited way of thinking. Now we *know* that we can exist in more than one way. We can converse mentally with Spirit that is not of the Earth plane.

It is comforting to know that we are constantly changing, and yet, stay the same, fundamentally. We are One. That is, we belong in *All That Is*. We take time to experience the Earth realm so that we may better know what it is that we are when we are unencumbered by Earth form. It is for us an experience that enlightens our way to be. We are forever grateful for this opportunity. We converse in this way so that we may know each other better. We are all part of the greater *Be*-ing that is God.

We know ourselves better when we experience each other in various relationships. Relationship is a mirror for our Souls. That is, we see ourselves reflected in the shining Light of other beings. We do this for each other so that we may grow and learn, so that we may manifest our dreams and hopes to experience that which we desire to experience.

Our hearts are open to new ways of *Be*-ing. It is for you to desire that this relationship go forward in time.

So be it.

Raymian

Our hearts
are filled with Love.
It is for us
a magnificent gift
that explodes
the myth
that we are evil.

I am interested in progressing, in seeing how this relationship can grow and be shared, so that we all can benefit from it. What would a new way of Be-ing, involving both worlds, be like?

It would comfort you to know that your Self does not end. It continues without form. It would help you in creating a more peaceful world knowing that material things matter least in the long run. It would provide you access to the knowledge of the ages, known forevermore. It would help you to know that you are never alone for we are always with you. It would create a dynamic relationship that can provide excitement and enthusiasm as you explore other realms while in Earth form.

It will bring you peace to know that you have tapped into your inner Source that is unlimited. It will help you to understand that you are more than Earth form, limited by that form and the characteristics you have chosen up-to-now to express in your Earthly *Be*-ing. You shall know your true Self, unlimited, expressive and wholly sacred.

So be it.

We are One. What you receive from me is generated by you and me together. We are One. There is no separation from Earth or Light Beings. We can be with *All That Is* every day, every night and forevermore.

Are we aspects of the same Self?

Yes, we are. And yet, we choose to separate in order to experience what that separation can teach us. We are Oneness.

Our hearts are filled with Love. It is for us a magnificent gift that explodes the myth that we are evil. We are Love, *only* Love.

If evil does exist, where does it come from?

It dwells in the hearts of those who don't believe Love is all there is. We have the capacity to shut down our Love-making, to become one without the core of Light-giving forces. We see only lack, lack of Love that permeates all that we do. We have shut down the mechanism that allows the Love to flow. Instead we have incubated fear, which is no more than Love confined. We suck up the love of external forces, but to no avail, for we cannot use the love of others to fill our emptiness, our lack of Love, our fear. We can only open our hearts to the Love that dwells within — so that the Love may flow and blend with all of the Love generated throughout the worlds.

Now we come to our part: It is to share Love with those who also want to partake in shared Love. Together we can create a world where we will all *know* that Love is of this world, for this world, and always has been available to all who live in the Earth realm.

So be it.

Raymian

Our hearts are open to Joy. Joy is Love expressed so clearly that we can know of nothing else that can compare. Our hearts reach out to all who know our ways are of the Soul, binding us together, now and forevermore.

Armand

We can be
with
each other,
not in body
but
in Soul.

11/18/00 4:30 p.m.
Rose River Conference Center, Virginia

I just realized that today is the anniversary of our wedding thirty-nine years ago. That is a long time ago, or is it really? We were so involved in guests and the Joy of the occasion. We cut the cake and fed each other for the first time as husband and wife. Our hearts were joined in witness on that day. We vowed to be together until death do us part. I could not imagine that happening as I said those words. It seemed so long away. But that was not so. Death came for you only sixteen years later.

And we did not part. Our Souls are joined. We can be with each other, not in body but in Soul. Our hearts seemed empty for awhile as we followed the way laid out for each of us. We did not know that we would come together again to continue relationship in another way.

We were told that relationships end at death. That was not so for me. I had to continue to what I thought was completion because your passing was so sudden. The opportunity to say "goodbye" was not there for me. Now I know that the goodbye is only temporary. We meet again.

You held me close to yourself because I was always there. It impedes the will to leave so soon. I missed the Earthly form for I, too, did not have the opportunity to tell you of my love for you and the girls.

It was ended far too soon for me. Life is a blessing bestowed on all of us. It is Love personified. I am one who enjoyed myself. We will love again in a new way, I told myself. That is true, for we love in many ways. From our hearts well up Loving thoughts. It is not only these thoughts that sustain us, but also our Love that generates the energy that we share.

So be it.

Raymian

We cannot continue
to hold onto
our grief
for things or people
that have passed on
to new ways
of Be-ing.

11/24/00 *at home*

Our hearts are open with Joy, Joy of knowing that *All That Is* is what we *are*. By that I mean, we Love each other throughout lifetimes. In silence we pray for life to continue as we have already known it. Instead we should embrace the unknown, for it is rich in experiences yet to be lived.

Our hearts are Joyous as we embrace the coming of each new day. For it is the beginning of new experiences that shall lead us toward knowing ourselves better than we now know each other. Our hearts are open to these experiences as we open our Selves to a new way of *Be*-ing.

As we look back on this lifetime we see may changes, shifts in attitude that have taken place. We know that tomorrow will not be like today because we approach it with a different attitude. We are entering a new way of *Be*-ing that is led by our attitude toward life-giving. We are approaching a way of being that is truly just that, a way of *Be*-ing. We cannot describe what that will be, because one must experience it rather than describe it. It *is*. That is it.

So be it.

We encounter forces that attempt to drive us off the center of our *Be*-ing. That is part of our experience, to stay centered in what and who we are. We must understand what forces are attempting to do. We cannot hold onto past ways and still be in the moment.

For us, that means we must move forward from this day to higher purposes. We cannot continue to hold onto our grief for things or people that have passed on to new ways of *Be*-ing. We look into our own Souls to see that which is meaningful to each of us, to all of us. Our hearts are open as we proceed.

You are gifted with knowing about the human condition. By that I mean, we love and are loved unless we block that Love from flowing forth. It is necessary to keep movement from becoming blocked or stuck, for that blocking prevents the free flow of energy along its path. We are One. We are one moving dynamic that is known to us as we are flowing with it. We cannot stay in only one way of *Be*-ing and live truly in this lifetime. We are compelled to follow along our path to regain knowledge of the Self which is *All That Is*.

So be it.

How can we "be" and "not be" at the same time?

It is for us a challenge to be unmoved by the forces that deter us, and at the same time flow with those that sweep us along the path on which we are meant to be. We are moving energy fields. We are not stopping our flow as we move through life. It is that we are unaffected by those forces that cause us to stray from our path. So we move in a state of *Be*-ing, though we are stilled. The stillness helps us to be aware of our *Be*-ing, to observe it interacting with life's forces.

We are enriched through experience. We are loved and are Loving each other. Together we gather energies along the path. We know each other more fully. We know our Selves, alone and together. Our journey is enriched by all who gather together to take a similar path for the time being. We feel each other's energy and are enriched.

As husband and wife we knew each other's foibles. We also gained strength from each other. We did what we thought was best for our family regardless of what others said. We were strong in our convictions and proceeded through life knowing and relying on our own inner sense of what was right for our children and us. The fruits have born us out. Our Love produced two wonderful women who Love in their own way. Their lives are enriched by the time that we all spent together.

When I left, you were faced with decisions about their future care. The path you followed was to trust in their judgment. We had instilled in our children a confidence that they would know what was right for each of them. No one else can interfere with the deep knowing of one's Self.

You were busy earning a living. We would have fared well if we had approached this together, but alone you managed well. The girls were not deprived of material gifts by my leaving. And they gathered strength from the challenges of "bringing themselves up." That was a favorite way that you described the growth process.

In the end we each are responsible for the way we mature. We share that responsibility with our parents, but each individual actually makes his or her own decisions about life's direction. Our daughters took hold of their own direction early in life, and did well. For they are the people that they are because of the decisions each of them made in their own lives.

It is true that I believed that each person is responsible for his or her own growth and development. I looked back on my own life and realized that my parents trusted me to make my own decisions. After all, what can a parent do except imbue a child with values that will provide guidance whenever there is a decision to be made.

As a youngster I was left on my own far more than children seem to be today. You also had to take responsibility early in life. You worked at the boarding house helping in whatever way you could. I helped in our family's business from the time I was very young. It was a challenge for me to process as many decks of cards as I could to earn my allowance. My father was a magician and in those days magicians had to create their own decks of magic cards.

That was our job. We both learned to work hard and to handle our own money. We transferred what we had experienced to our children. They were responsible for helping out and handling their allowance.

We had a big garden. You worked in the garden during the summer when you were home from teaching school. I planted the garden in the early spring and harvested in the fall. It was healthy living, growing almost all that we ate. Our cupboards and freezer were full, as were our hearts, for we all worked together as a family to produce our largess.

Now there is little visible left of from all that cultivating. The gardens are long gone, overgrown with weeds. We no longer have well manicured lawns or flowers to pick. Disrepair has claimed the arbor. Only the rocks put in place by your labor remain hidden, by weeds overgrown.

But that is not the true picture. For beneath it all stands a family well grown. The weeds matter not, for it is what we take with us that counts. We have grown strong and true to our destined ways. We can look back and see that choices allowed the weeds to grow, as hearts and Souls prospered. We chose to grow the human Spirit, to Love and be loved. The garden of our Soul-growth has blossomed. It may not be visible on the landscape, but it is the Light that shines forth from our hearts.

Raymian

Know that life
is a test,
a place to learn
this way of Be-ing
regardless
of the circumstances.

11/26/00   *at home*

Raymian, let us continue...

We are as our hearts are. We continue in Loving ways as we write this missive. We know that the world is changing. It is evolving. And we are evolving along with our worlds.

So be it.

Today we begin with knowing our Joy is our expression. We are Loving beings. We sometimes have a difficult time expressing that Love. We get bound up in everyday things and ways that prevent us from flowing smoothly. That is, we have preconceived ideas about the way to go instead of flowing and watching what appears before us as opportunities. We know that life is a path. Sometimes we diverge form the way laid out before us. That is O.K. for we will resume our way as we progress.

Our hearts are open to many ways of *Be*-ing. That is, we can express our *Be*-ingness in many ways. We do not sit on a stump and watch the world go by without in some way contributing our energies to the flow. When we are consumed with tasks, we are flowing along as if tied up in brambles — bound by sharp pointed bushes that keep us from being free to express ourselves. We must let loose the branches that prevent us from moving forward in a free and open way. We *are* Love. The Loving energy expressed can free us from anything that appears to bind our energies.

Our course is to Love those who are hateful so that we may proceed. The Joy that is expressed is held with Loving ways. Notice what happens internally when you are disturbed. Your clarity erodes and you feel bound by the energies that would normally flow forth. Be One with *All That Is* and you are released from the strings that tie you to old ways of thinking.

Our hearts are then open to new ways of thinking and *Be*-ing. You ask, "What are those new ways?" To be One with *All That Is* is to experience your Self without boundries. To be One is to Love fully, to be filled with Love that leaks out, brimming over from the deep well within. Know that life is a test, a place to learn this way of *Be*-ing regardless of the circumstances.

We have come a long way in the twenty-three years since I left the Earth plane. In the times when we were together on Earth people did not express Love freely. We were bound by appropriate ways of behaving in public. There was very little touching. Men could shake hands, but a man did not extend his hand to a woman unless she did so first. Very few women shook hands with anyone. Hugs were not generally accepted either. We kept our distance from each other.

During that time some of the churches began exchanging greetings of peace. People actually turned toward each other at an appointed time and greeted the people on either side of them, as well as those in the pews in front and behind. This was a beginning step in reaching out to others, including them in one's personal space. We had to learn to let go of our boundries.

I remember what a difficult time I had connecting with people. Part of it was upbringing and part of it was something in me that sent a signal to others that I did not want to embrace. All that changed when you died.

The grief was so strong that an embrace was the only way to communicate caring and Oneness in our overwhelming sadness. We had lost a father, teacher, community servant, son, brother, friend, husband and more. We shared our Loving sorrow by coming together in Joy for the life that you lived, the life we all lived with you. I remember feeling that I now know what Love is, as I felt the combined energies of all who attended your funeral. I had crossed over a barrier that melted away from the Love I felt.

What lessons do we learn from experiences like this?

Only that Love fills voids created when one leaves this planet. We hold onto memories and fill ourselves with grief. We can let go of personhood and dwell instead in Love. We have not left you without Love. The Loving energy continues throughout lifetimes. We change form but our Love for each other is eternal. And now we begin anew to reassemble a lifetime of Love lived, through you, without boundries.

We cannot hold back our Love. Our Love must be expressed. On these pages you and I are sharing our love with *All That Is*. We know that our hearts' desire is to know each other in a new way. Our memories only show that shared experience reinforces that which we already know.

Our hearts are bound together. That is not the same as boundries that keep us from expressing ourselves. This binding together is without ties, for we are boundless energy. We are free to express our hopes and dreams, to manifest and to experience ways of *Be*-ing. I am no longer in form; therefore, my way of *Be*-ing is not the same as yours. Yet we can communicate, share past memories and know that the future is bright.

We shall continue this way of communicating *for the time being.* That has more than one meaning!

Our hearts are stretched as we discuss our feelings. We keep hidden our feelings even from our Selves. That has the effect of stymieing our growth. It is better to share our deepest feelings than to let that Love be unexpressed.

So be it.

"I love you" is one way of expressing feelings. Among other ways is service to others, caring, smiling, sharing thoughts, playing musical instruments, singing, painting, etc. All of these are methods of communicating. We choose our media as our energy is expressed. Ours is a simple *Be*-ing. Just being with One another melds our energies and expresses togetherness. There is no disharmony to deplete our energies. It is boundless as we fill the void from our Source.

Raymian

*We know
that there is
another way of Be-ing
that is not confined
to the form we take
in this Earth life..*

11/30/00 *at home*

Our hearts are boundless, that is, we fly through space that is unbounded. We know that there is another way of *Be*-ing that is not confined to the form we take in this Earth life. Our hearts are able to communicate with *All That Is,* now and forevermore. We know this. We have begun to experience this more in our awareness.

We are overjoyed at the potential that this communication takes us to new ways of knowing and *Be*-ing. It is boundless. We have just begun to explore its potential. Just when we think that we have accumulated so much information, we find that we have not really begun to access the potential knowledge that already exists! This will blow your mind, but not your heart, for the heart's energy is eternal and universal.

We know that our journey will unfold in a new way. We will meld both worlds in pursuit of the Joy we are meant to *be* and to express. All is hopeful.

So be it.

Armand

12/2/00 at home

Our hearts are open to finding our way in this new way of *Be*-ing. It is open to speculation that we will find our hearts' desire within our own Spirit. By that I mean, we have accumulated much. For us that is a sign of richness and power. We flame our hearts desire with hopes for accumulating more. That is as we have been told and as we hear ourselves talk about the things we want to do or have.

"What's new?" is a favorite greeting. We ask what's new because we don't want to hear that which we have already heard. That is so in greeting people. But that is not so in our every day ways of living.

We hear within the same tapes running day after day. We respond to each episode in life the same way we have always responded. It takes much effort to stop the cycle of sameness, of redundancy, that binds us to what is the old way. And yet we encourage our children to repeat over and over again the same responses that they have learned. How can we learn a new way when we prefer to participate in reruns?

Raymian

How can we learn
a new way
when we prefer
to participate
in reruns?

12/3/00 *at home*

I feel detached from this writing. It is a way to tell my story. And yet, when the words are laid to the paper, it takes on a different meaning, or no meaning.

What has been said, has been said for all who care to listen.

Each day that I sit and record the voices within, I know not what the message will be. Much of it is a mixture of my thoughts and experience, and it is also a new way of expressing that which I have known. Nothing is "new." It is just restated in a new way. It is combined in a new way. The many swirling thoughts and memories are reassembled to tell my story, our story, today.

It is a cleansing experience in that unexpressed thoughts are allowed to float to the page, reform themselves in the air, and drop into place much like the letters forming words in scrabble. The potential for these combinations is always there. But we are dealt a limited amount of letters. These are what we must use in combination with those laid out before to make new words. We are limited in the game by its rules, and yet the potential combinations are truly unlimited. That is the way it is in life. We are limited only by the rules we agree to live by. We can change the game, and we can change the rules. Be not limited. Seek "new" ways to be unlimited by our past experiences. The potential is truly unlimited.

Our hearts are open to new ways of *Be*-ing. We can begin again. As a matter of fact we do begin again with each and every moment. What is past is past. That is so.

So be it.

Our path is one of Love fulfilled. That is, we hear the voices of our hearts speaking to us. These many voices are with us always. Do you Love yourself enough to listen to the voices that speak to you? You say, "yes."

Hear what I have to say: Love abounds both *in* you and *around* you. You are bathed in a sea of Loving. Enjoy the waves! Enjoy the Lightness being buoyed up by Love! Enjoy the sparkling beads of light bounced off the water's surface. Come up for air and you will find Love permeates all of the world. You cannot elude the forces of Love. They are *you*. You *are* Love.

Try to love, and you will stymie Love, for *trying* cloaks Love. It smothers the natural flow by setting up barriers, imaginary barriers. There are no barriers to Love except those that we create ourselves.

Our hearts are open to Love flowing forth. We are joined in this endeavor. We hold our hearts open. Test yourself to see if you truly believe this. When you feel your heart closing down, absorb the hurt and transform it to Love. You must believe that the Love is so strong *within* that nothing can survive in any form that is not Love. *All* is Love.

So be it.

And now, in the name of Love, I give you Raymian.

Hello again! The energy is lighter when I am here with you. It is because we have known each other in form. Our hearts are bound together in eternal Love.

The message today has at its core Love. That can be the only way, for we *are* Love. It is hard to understand this when we are confronted with many energies that appear not to be Love. But *all* is Loving-energy. It is what we *do* with it that makes it appear otherwise.

We compel our hearts to close down out of fear of being hurt. As we protect ourselves, we counter our natural ways of *Be*-ing. It is a trick we play on ourselves. Who else has the fortitude to assemble a wall so high, and so low, that can block all energies from reaching us?

The effect of that wall is also to block our own energy of Love from flowing outward. That is the situation which so many of us have created for ourselves: a wall so thick that we are isolated in our own Loving being. But like the candle that burns in a jar, we can burn brightly until the lid is closed. That act completely cuts off life-giving oxygen, and the flame that once burned brightly dies. So it is with us. If we build the wall of protection too airtight, our Light will dim and smolder.

We cannot cut ourselves off completely and expect to continue to express Love, for there is nowhere where the Love can expand when it is confined tightly. Love moves beyond the bounds when it is allowed to flow. One must not hold back Love for it will build within in an unhealthy way. Our Love was unexpressed when we did not tell each other of the faults we found.

Raymian

There are no barriers
to Love
except those
that we create
ourselves.

12/10/00   at home

Raymian, are you there?

I am. I Love you. We are One as we reach out to tell our story. We come from our hearts as we tell tales of being One. Our hearts are open.

Today is a day of Love. You have moved to a new level of Love-giving that is knowing yourself better than before. Our hearts know what it is that we need to express as we go forth.

So be it.

Raymian

12/16/00   at home

Today I begin with new lightness. I am entering a period of respite away from work. I must ready the house for our children to come home. We will all be here: Our daughters, their husbands, and our three grandsons -- the boys you always wanted. On Friday we will all go to see my mother. She is grieving the loss of my dad.

Let her know that all is well. Our hearts are open to a way of *Be*-ing that permeates all of our doing.

I am shifting to concentrate on them. It is indeed a gift of themselves that they are coming here. You and I had sixteen Christmases together. It was fun when you dressed up as Santa to entertain the kids at school. I remember leading the kids in song, and as the girls grew older, they dressed up in red and green and became Santa's helpers.

You planned the faculty party. That was where you were the evening when you left, planning the faculty party at a restaurant. It was October. The leaves were brilliant oranges and yellows. Thoughts of changing the decor to red and green had not yet entered most people's minds. But you were planning the holiday party.

I don't remember whether I went to that party. I know that we went away for the holidays. I was getting ready to start a new job with the extension service. I had been substitute teaching in November and December to bring in some money. My thoughts were primarily on finding a way to support the family.

I remember going to the State Unemployment Office. The counselor told me that I probably could get a job earning $10,000 per year, if I was lucky. That was less than half of what you were earning as a teacher for twenty-five years. But he went on to say that if I worked at it, I could be earning what you had in three to five years. At the end of three full years, I reached my goal!

I reached other goals, too. Our children grew strong and wise. They are wonderful women. They have some of your characteristics and some of mine. They are good parents. They love their children and blend their value systems with those of their husbands. Today fathers take a good deal more responsibility for their children than most men did in our time, although you shared that responsibility with me.

12/17/00   at home

Raymian. Where are you?

I am here beside you. We love to play games. That is, I have been about to call, but was not sure you were ready. I see you are cleaning house. It is time to divest yourself of old things. It is like refreshing yourself with nothing to hold on to.

You are One with *All That Is*. It is a dilemma when you have to think about discarding something that you think you might need. We *need* very little. We grasp at that which presents itself to us, and then save, save, save. We are not meant to hold onto things. As we flow through life we may temporarily hold onto debris that floats along beside us. But that, too, has its own path.

We mortals hold on tenaciously. When will we learn that we cannot hold onto anything for we are Light moving through the universe? We become unburdened as we discard that which we have accumulated. We have talked much about accumulated memories. Remember not all that has gone past. Instead, sense the past connection by accessing the Universal Being. We all *know* everything. It is not that we have to remember, it is that we can access *All That Was, Is and Will Be*.

So be it.

Raymian

When will we learn
that we cannot
hold onto anything
for we
Are Light
moving through the universe?

12/24/00   at home

I am here to tell you that you are One with *All That Is*. We play with each other from time to time. It is that we are always here to be Love that is shared.

Our daughters and their families brought much Love to this house. It has been empty of that Love for a long time. Their visit this week returned the vibes of Love at a new level. We are proud of their accomplishments, but even more so of the lives they lead. For they demonstrate a well integrated life of Love and work, fun and enjoyment.

We are here to benefit the lives of others, as well as our Selves. That means we know that our job is to instill in our offspring an appreciation of one another. Our hope is that this Light of appreciation will glow brighter as one defines oneself in the ways of the world.

We know that life is a series of Loves. By that I mean, we Love one another as we progress through the pathway of life. Along the way we encounter many obstacles that can delay or defray our efforts. Think not, "What we are saying?," only *know* what is said here.

We know what is meant to be. We must access that vision or feeling to *know* what is meant to be. To do this, *know* that all is One. That is the clue to knowing *All That Is*. By that I mean, we *are*, and yet we do not *know* what *is*. For we look in the wrong places for confirmation of what *is*. We shall *know*, without doubt, what *is*, as we proceed through this life.

So be it.

Tell me more of the "series of loves."

It is for us a metaphor for the way that we approach life. We love and leave one stranded without the love of another. That is our way of moving from one relationship to another. You know what I mean. We encounter other human beings temporarily in this lifetime. And yet, we move on to another relationship. For a while our energies are combined, not separated. As we move into another's energy field we cannot help but be affected by them. Our energies mingle. They do not separate completely upon leaving. We will know more of these encounters as we proceed.

And now, I come to you with Love of the ages. For we have know each other's energies for eons. We Love without boundries. That is true about our relationship now and before, as well as after, as all Earth beings refer to Time. Our message today is to Love thy Self as much as you can, for you are alone in the generation of loving energy for your Self. It is not that there is no other source; it is that you are your primary Source.

We are all One. It is our way to *be*. You must learn to access this Oneness wherever you are and whenever you want to. We mean that you can know of that which we speak, even as you go about your daily routine. It is Love that is always available to you, *no matter what.* You can access that Love at every juncture, no matter where or when. This is a learning for many who think that one must be in some special place at some special time to access Love*ness*.

And now, I bid you adieu, for you have matters to attend to.

Ramón

I Love you.

It is Love
that is always
available to you,
no matter what.

12/26/00   at home

Tomorrow I go to India. Before I leave I want to say how much I have enjoyed this communication. I noticed that when I am with different groups of people my desire and ability to record our sayings is limited and sometimes stops for a while. Can you tell me more about this?

We know when we want to communicate. Sometimes we are totally involved in the day-to-day activities, and this type of writing would interfere with your being totally involved. That is why we are separate for a while. It is not complete separateness but rather a "knowing" that one's communication may interfere with *Be*-ing totally in one moment.

Of course, that is not so, because we can be in more than one dimension at a time. That is the point of this communication. It can be accessed at any time, no matter what you are doing. It is that your attention may wander when you are trying to be in another dimension while acting in the Time dimension. Therefore, we pick our times of communication carefully.

It is also true that the vibrations of others affect you. We have spoken of that earlier. When your energies meld, it superficially affects the energy around you. You can also feel it in your heart. When we were together on Earth our energies were melded. We could communicate without words. We knew what each other would say or do. That is the total knowing that is associated with human activities.

Our hearts are open to developing our communication skills in a way not previously thought possible in everyday life. We are blind to the sights that exist in other dimensions. But we know that those things that we cannot see exist.

So be it.

Our communication this year began around the time of your return from the Southern Hemisphere. We welcomed the light of the new dawn off the coast of New Zealand in a ceremony conducted by the Maori. The ceremony was broadcast around the world as a harbinger of the new Light of the new millennium shining on us.

We also have hopes of the Light permeating all things, all ways, and Love becoming brighter. It is for us a new dawning, too, for we are again in constant communication. We know that you are dedicated to recording this communication that it, too, may see the light of a new dawning. To tell tales of writing with Spirit is your way of knowing that all is well within and without.

Our hearts are strong. For they have grown through our experiences. To see the dawn is a metaphor of life-giving forces being revealed. We know that you are a student of Light in this lifetime. You will now go forth to dawn in another land, a place where these communications have existed for eons. You will learn of Light-giving forces that are around you. You will know that all of which we speak is indeed held as true in other cultures. Our hope is that you will proceed with Love and Light as your guides.

So be it.

And now, I give you Raymian who is Spirit guide to you in this lifetime, and you to him, as he continues to grow through this correspondence.

Armand

Today is the last day that you will have this communication this year. You are off to other activities abroad. It is fitting that we say adieu in a way that means that we shall return to this form of communication afterward. Our hearts are filled with much to say. Our hopes include being able to convey these thoughts to others. Whether that be so or not, we will always be together in our venture.

We have a little matter to cover. It is about the Love that still exists after death. Our hearts are separated for a while. That is necessary for healing. Fundamentally we are alone no more, but we feel as though we have been deserted. It is natural to feel loss. We have lost the human element. It is the form and its animal energies that are gone. But the essence remains. That is why we can feel another person's presence when they are absent in form. We know that they are here, and yet we are told that they are gone and there can be no communication with them. It is true that our bodies decay or are otherwise disposed of. But we are *not* our bodies.

We are Soul, the essence of *Be*-ing that lives on after death. We can communicate with you forevermore, now and beyond this lifetime. We know that we *are* Love. It is Love that lingers on, whether you wish it to be there or not. We come from the highest dimension of Light. We are *all* Light. It is for you to remember that Light shines through you. It cannot be hidden, for you *are* Love everlasting. Our hearts are Love. That is all. It shall be known to you, and to me, that Love permeates *All That Is*. There is nothing else, only Love.

So be it.

Our hearts are open to new ways for the communication of Love. It is these words that can reveal a way of Love sharing beyond the dimensions. I only *know* that this is so now that I have passed over to another dimension. I was not clear about this on Earth. As a matter of fact, I scoffed at the thought of it.

You, too, were unsure. It was only with my passing that you became a seeker of knowing. It was not necessarily a consequence of my passing, but only a way that revealed new ways of looking at those things that we were taught.

You knew that there was something else that you were not taught. The feelings were not explained by everyday knowledge. Coincidences could not be explained in normal ways. And last, the ability to write that came so easily at an appointed moment, the night before a paper was due, haunted you throughout your adulthood. How do these things happen? How can we make them happen when we want to?

It has been a search that has led you to this moment, a moment of anticipation about the trip to India. Will you be able to explain the unexplainable when you return? Or will it be a trip filled with information, insights and experience unique to you? We will see. It is only one day away. I look forward to continuing this journey and sharing it with you.

Raymian

Part Three

Shifting Relationship

It is a softening
of the inner being
that takes place
when the heart's strings
need loosening.

12/29/00 Madras/Chennai, India in Church of St Mary

We loved each other so much that we wed in an Episcopal Church. It is Love that permeates these walls and our hearts. We know that Love is binding our hearts to its cause. Be with me always in this endeavor.

1/05/01 Tirumvannamalai, India at Sri Ramana Mahjarishi Asramam

Sri Ramana, what say you?

Only that I *am.* I have said that many times. I am that I *am.* I am not my body. I am not my senses. I *am.* You are what you *are.* Your inquiry into what you *are* is your path. It is so that you may return to the essential Self. The Self is *All That Is.*

To access the conscious awareness, one must still one's Self. That is, the ego-self must be put aside to deepen awareness. It is for you a conscious journey for you know your way to *All That Is.* It is for us to stay there in the knowing as we complete our time on Earth. It is for you a journey that has brought you to this place. This is a haven for those seeking the Truth. Enlightenment is knowing who you *are*. It is listening to the voice within the mind that tells you what *is*. For it is a journey of many steps. Keep quiet and you, too, shall know of what I speak.

Our hearts are open. Our hearts are Source. It is our heart that speaks to us to know *All That Is*. Follow the heart's words. Speak with that which is felt *within*. Know mindfulness, for it is together that one can come to know one's Self.

Speak not of these words on this trip. Wait and see what develops afterwards.

You may go to the hilltop or you may sit here to tell the story in your writing. It matters not where you are, for you *are* everywhere, and everywhere is within you. And now I bring you Raymian.

I am here to say that you have traveled far on Earth. It is an accomplishment that I never sought for I was afraid to fly. Little did I know that I would be light and airy where there is no distinction like flying!

Our hearts are joined even when you have traveled halfway around the Earth. We know no bounds. We are everywhere, too. Our lesson today is that no matter where you are, you *are*.

So be it.

I am inclined to be Joyful at knowing that you are finding a way to be in this lifetime that surpasses the time we had together. Your path was different from mine in that you had to go much of it alone.

Our time together laid a foundation of family, of intimacy and a loving supportive group. Together we accomplished a lot. The children were born, and have now grown. Our hearts' desire has been accomplished. And now we have another chore. It is to write a book of Love letters that let everyone know that life is temporary and relationships continue after death.

We leave our bodies, but not our heart's Source. It is from that Source that we gain the life-like tendencies. We are forevermore a maiden and her lover. We know that life is short and that we should touch the heart of all Souls that we encounter.

So be it.

And now, I return you to Ramana for some parting words.

I am that I *am*, as you are, as you *are*. Our heart Source is the way to know who you *are*. Know your Source and you will know *you*.

So be it.

Sri Ramana, you say "do not seek the dead," and yet you brought me Raymian. Why?

Because you are supposed to do this task. Others may learn from it. But it is not helpful in reaching the Supra Spirit level. You will know the Spirit, but the writing is only comforting to those who wish to speak with the dead. To be One with *All That Is* is the ultimate. To speak with the dead is comforting. I know that Love is *All That Is*. So do you. That is all.

I came to you knowing that Love is supreme. We know our hearts' desire is to Love. And now, I bring you Raymian, the guide of this lifetime, to be with you, now and forevermore.

I am here to be with you because we Loved each other in this lifetime and many more. Our hearts are joined. By that I mean, we are of one Source. We cannot separate. We must...

(interrupted to move on with the tour)

It matters not
where you are,
for you Are
everywhere,
and everywhere
is within you.

01/10/01 4:30 p.m.
returning to New York via Brussels

Our hearts are open. There stands before us a new day of liberation from not knowing who we *are*. It is written that you are Love. Love is sublime. You may know this instinctively or you may find this Truth in a lifelong search.

Our hearts are our Source of Love. That is, we are that which we *are*. Our hearts speak to us with renewed wisdom. It is for you to continue with your writing. It is a blessing bestowed. Our hearts shall guide us in our endeavors. Be not afraid to Love again. It is hopeful that you will proceed to your destiny.

So be it.

Denice, our time together was short. We had one another as mates. We Loved with our hearts, minds and Souls. It is true that we exist still in the sands of time and we will, forevermore.

Raymian

It should be said
that these relationships
are special
but they should
Not
take the place
of those lived
in daily life on Earth.

01/15/01   *at home*

I have been hesitant to begin again with our writing in the New Year. Let us begin.

I am here, waiting to begin our Love letters. We have known for some time that this is a way of knowing that should be shared with others. Our sharing is important in that it shows all others that it is possible to communicate beyond the veil of death. We can continue as we have or we can accelerate the letters.

I am hoping that we can move forward more rapidly. I am willing to devote the time and energy to it.

Our form is what we see on Earth. It is a reminder to us of our human condition. What we hear does not carry with it the same physicality. I could be in the next room, halfway around the world or in another dimension. You quiet yourself down and listen within to the voices of the heart speaking to you. You can conjure up a physical form to go with the voice or just see whatever you choose. That is the lesson for today: to know what you are hearing is true to your way of *Be*-ing, just as is your sight and hearing in physical form.

We encounter many beings through our hearts' center. We use discernment on allowing those beings to enter into our consciousness. That is what you have chosen to do. Our communication is heartfelt. We know each other on many levels. This is only one of these levels.

Our story is one of hopefulness. We endeavor to claim communication with loved ones who have passed on. It is true that we can access not only memories but also ongoing relationships. It should be said that these relationships are special but they should not take the place of those lived in daily life on Earth. They supplement that which you *know* and Love in the world realized.

We chose to share our communications so that all may know it is possible to continue in knowing one another beyond the realm in which you now exist. It is for us a completion of a promise made before we came into this life. It is time that all who care to know or to exercise their gift may do so. It is comforting to know that life forms continue to exist after physical death.

So be it.

And now let us continue our dialog, for we have much to say. Our hearts are open in a way that allows communication between the dimensions. That is meant to be a way to tell your story so that others, too, may hear their own story being told. We must continue in this way until such time that we have satisfied our being One with each other.

By "continue in this way" I mean that we will share our hearts' desires. That is to be one who knows *All That Is*. We must center ourselves in the divine. It is for us a way to *be*. Our hearts are open; our minds are closed to the chatter that so much occupies our time on Earth. To be purely in a state of *Be*-ing is to be open to that which *is*, that which flows through us.

We are meant to be in a state of equilibrium so that we may manifest that which is on Earth. Our hearts' desire is to be in this state so that we may be One, forevermore. Our lessons are taught as we move in and out of this state of *Be*-ing. We are forever challenged to leave this state, to be distracted. Center on your Source of *Be*-ing and you shall know of that which I speak.

Raymian

To be purely
in a state
of Be-ing
is to be
Open
to that which Is,
that which
flows through us.

01/19/01   *at home*

What is the saying that I remember so well? "Love is for us caring and knowing that the other cares for us." We are as caring today as we were when on Earth, together. That is, we know each other so well that we care for each other in ways that no one else could possibly know. Our hearts' are drawn together as we proceed with these writings. Today we shall talk of Love that permeates *All That Is*. We are fortunate to have known each other in form. Not all beings have that opportunity. We care what happens when we remember the Love shared between us.

Our hearts are open again and again. That is, we tend to close ourselves to others from time to time. It is not easy to stay open to another. You are having such difficulty now. I sense that you feel that these writings are moving slowly and are not of great importance. That is so because we stray from our intended mission by our daily distractions. It is not easy to sit in the evening and converse in this way.

You are right! I think that we are stuck. There is nothing new coming that is profound. It is becoming a chore rather than a pleasure to converse. I'd like to know where this writing is going to take us, as well as those with whom we share these words.

Be not concerned over the end result. Just commit to continuing the sessions for we will make progress, as you are meant to.

So be it.

That's easier said than done. I want to feel inspired, as well as feel like I'm doing something worthwhile!

01/22/01   at home

It is for us a letter of Love that we share with each other and all who want to read these words. We are embarking on a new adventure, the end of which we do not now know. Our hearts are joined in this venture. That is all that we know.

Our senses are heightened as we share our thoughts. The senses of which I speak are not the ordinary senses with which we know daily life. These are enhanced senses that help us to communicate across worlds.

We know that we are not sharing the same existence in the same way. You are in form and I am Spirit, without body. We share communication, but little else, for your world is density that guides your everyday movements. I am Spirit which is free to wander throughout the universe, only communicating with those in your realm who wish to tune in.

It is wonderful to be able to keep tabs on your daily activities. But I only do this with your permission. For we are alone in our endeavors only when we wish to be alone. A tumultuous crowd wishes you well. But only a few of us actually get to participate in that part of your life where you enable us to. It is your desire to continue to communicate that allows these sessions to continue. I know that you desire to share these messages, as do I.

Our first hope is to stem the label that is often applied to this type of work. It is not clairvoyant or clairaudient in the way that some say predicts the future. We do not do that. We share our desires for the radiating of Love between the worlds. We know that Love permeates all, including barriers between the worlds. Our hope is to share Love that is everlasting.

So be it.

And now I give you one who is waiting to communicate with you. It is a surprise, for it is one whom you have known before. I bring you William, whom you have known before.

What is your message?

Love is forever. I have known only Love since I joined forces with *All That Is*.

So be it.

And now, I have Love letters for you.

You are my heart and my Soul joined in Love. I have always known that we would part in the Earthly way, but this is greater than all could have imagined. Love is permeating everything that I say and do. It is Love sublime. I know that you can feel that of which I speak. Know that the best is yet to come.

Raymian

Love

*is an energy
that seeks to expand.*

1/31/01   *at home*

I am here to tell you that Love is immortal. You say that Love
lingers, forevermore. That is so. We Love with our hearts' desire.
That is, it is meant to be that we share our Love with all there is.

Our hearts are open. We feel for each other a Love that
permeates all else. That is, we are not aware that our Love is felt
by all-else. We favor our intimates with our Love, but all others
who encounter us also feel the Love that we radiate.

We are beings of Light. That Light shines forth through all kinds
of circumstances. We are known to have Love-Light that shines
without shining. Instead, it is detected by our senses in other
ways. We sense, we *know* without someone telling us that there
is Love flowing between us. We know by our own inner
knowing. We are aided by our uncanny ability to pick up vibrant
expressions of Love.

We also feel Love withdrawn. That is the condition that is set up
when one is afraid. We withdraw the radiance. We hold back the
flow, the natural flow of Love bearing energies. We dam the
Love; hold it back, saving it for some future encounter, or so we
think. But Love that does not flow can be destructive. It is
welling up behind a barrier created within us. Sometimes the
dam bursts forth with such powerful energy that it seeks to
destroy that which it Loves.

Anger is such an example. Originally Love, caring for another,
that has been held back but continues to build, knows no other

way of expressing itself other than to gush forth with such fury that all that Love becomes destructive. It is better to flow forth remembering that Love is an energy that seeks to expand. It should not be confined behind barriers of disappointment. We care for ourselves as we care for others. We must remember that Love permeates *All That Is*. It moves beyond all barriers unless there is a deliberate attempt to hold it back.

We say that withdrawal of Love is not deliberate. We fear the consequences if we allow ourselves to experience fully the Love we generate. We know that our thoughts govern our actions. We pile all of these causes into one bundle of Love that is welling within, but cannot get out of our hearts.

We say that Love is *within* us. We know that. But we cannot feel the Love that is blocked. Many people have been in a state of holding back for so long that they cannot imagine what it would be like to allow their pent up energies the freedom to flow forth. It is a lesson in allowance.

The Love is there in abundance. The gates must be gradually spread apart to allow first a trickle, then a stream, and finally an unencumbered flow that spreads beyond the boundries so long confining. It is a loosening of our grip on ourselves. It is a relaxed effort, an *effortlessness* that we are seeking. We can be in a level of consciousness that allows our hearts to open fully.

Raymian

We now know
that Love
does just that —
it allows us
to flow through
all adversity.

1/31/01   at home in the evening

I've been thinking about the many years when I held back the Love from flowing. People would say, "Open your heart." But I did not know what they meant or what that would feel like. To be solid and firm in my conviction that stoicism was the way to be was, for me, strength. How could I be any other way but strong and stoic?

It is a softening of the inner being that takes place when the heart's strings need loosening. It is relaxation in the place of resistance. We cannot understand how strength can be derived from softening the blow, allowing deflection rather than headstrong resistance. We were socialized to be firm in our convictions, to allow no one to deter our way. We now know that Love does just that. It allows us to flow through all adversity. It compels us to take the lead in our own lives. It moves us forward, not on our terms but on all terms that help us to be ourselves — Selves that are not created from an ideal picture, but rather evolve from the heart. We know that we are beings who Love one another. We seldom act that way.

So be it.

And now I bring you Raymian, the guiding Light of your self-fulfilling ways.

I am here to say that we are forever propelled forward. What holds us back is our self-fulfilling ways. We are, as we said, "We will be."

And now I give you William.

Denice, I know you wonder who I am. I am one whom you have known before.

(William was my meditation teacher who passed over two years ago).

It is our way to contact those who are open. We are beings of Light, Love and hope. We come to you in sincerity to allay fears for the future. The future is bright. It can only be that way. Hope is for us a crutch that we do not need, for we shall see brightness wherever we go on Earth, as in the heavens.

So be it.

And now, I bring back Raymian, the father of your children, and the lover of *All That Is.*

Why is William coming to speak?

He is anxious to carry messages of hope and understanding to the world. He is helping to convey that Love is *All That Is.* I am here to bring messages that can be understood by you and many others. Together we shall share our Love with the world.

And now, I bring you one who is trying to contact your mother. It is her brother who passed from the Earth many years ago. His message is of Love for a childhood sister who helped him. He says that Love is eternal, now and forevermore.

The end of this missive is near. We have done many things together. This is as important as anything we did before. May you love the times we spent together, both in this way and on Earth.

Does this mean all the writing is finished?

No, only our hearts' work with the missive will continue as it was before. I look forward to continuing in the way.

I think I am afriad that the work together will end before we have told all there is to tell. Please don't play with words in such a way that I will get that idea.

Our hearts
are formed
within the shell
of our body
on Earth,
but
there is no limit
to their depth or breadth.

2/4/01 at home

Now, I give you Raymian.

Our hearts are bound within, not without. By that I mean, we Love each other boundlessly. Our hearts are formed within the shell of our body on Earth, but there is no limit to their depth or breadth.

"Our home is where our heart is." That is not just a saying, but also a Truth. We live our lives in many places. But our home is with us, no matter where we are. You have known many places. But your heart has sustained you wherever you are.

It is not place that makes one feel at home. It is Loving feelings comforting us in familiar surroundings, as well as those places that are strange to us. We like the familiar. But we thrive on the unknown. We seek a combination of nurturing at home, as well as stimulation from new places and experiences. Balancing the two will make for a fruitful and creative lifetime.

Later that same day

We know that our time together is limited. We have felt Love seeking our hearts' desire. We know that we shall always *be* Love. That is so.

So be it.

You find it difficult to render words to paper in a lot of situations. That is not unusual for we all have difficulty confining our communication power to paper. It is easier to write in the sky than it is to sit in one place and contemplate an empty screen or a blank piece of paper.

Our hearts are not confined to words written on paper. That is a form of expression that is governed by man-made rules. In the real world, there are no tablets. There are only thoughts of Love that permeate *All That Is*. To try to express or describe this phenomenon is for us an extremely difficult task. It is confining something that cannot be confined, only expressed.

Raymian

2/7/01 at home

Our hearts are open. It is the heart that is the center of one's *Be*-ing. We are forever trying to access our Source that *is* and *comes* from the heart Source. We shall always know that our hearts are joined in Love. It is noble to think otherwise, for we are creatures of habit who must display our heart's energy so that others may know who we are. By that I mean, we display our moods so that we convey that all is or is not well with us.

Our hearts' desire is that others know who we truly *are*. To many of us that means displaying the dark side, as well as the Light. We ponder our future, telling those we know about our plans. It is for us a display of our hopes. We are forever sharing our thoughts with others, trying to let them know what it is that we are feeling.

It is so difficult to truly communicate with another person when we use words. Words are our means of story telling. And yet there are other ways to communicate that are so subtle that most of us overlook them. It is our dreams that convey our innermost thoughts. We are open to deliberating in our sleep. We say that we are sleeping when we are indeed very active.

What is the point of this communication?

It is to tell us of more subtle ways of *Be*-ing. It is to convey that we are always letting others know how we feel or think by gentle rocking waves conveyed without speaking. We do not need to speak to communicate with another. We merely convey our thoughts and feelings through the ethers. It is so. We are adept at this form of communication. We pick up signals from each other. It is not as blatant as semaphore, but rather a sensing without words. We *know*.

You and I knew what each other would value. We did not need to discuss many things. We just knew and could act on it. Part of this was shared values. When two people have similar upbringing, their value systems are likewise similar. We seek out people who share our values. We are most comfortable with them. It is not surprising that we are still sharing those same values. It is what we believe in. It is the basis on which we make our choices.

Raymian

What we believe
can dilute
what we truly Are.

2/9/01   at home

I am wondering what choices we have to make now.

It is as if we were together sometimes. My heart is joined with yours. We know that life is sweeter for us when we can share with another. It is that we are now alone most of the time. We share whenever we like. Otherwise, we pretend that there is no one else there. Our hearts are joined so that we may continue to write of Love that lasts beyond the grave. It is nonsense that we perish, for we are One, now and forevermore.

What you are experiencing in your day-to-day life is changing relationships. As you move from place to place you encounter many people. Our hearts are open to meeting and greeting these Souls each day. We are fortunate to go forth with Love in our hearts to meet and greet. We must know that these relationships appear to be temporary. Indeed, they are not.

We meet people who seem to be first-time acquaintances. But we are all connected. We have known and/or will know each other again in Spirit just like you and me. We knew each other before our experience together on Earth and we know each other now, even though one of us is not in body. We decided that we would embark upon this work to help all who will listen to listen to their hearts and know of what we speak.

Raymian

2/19/01 at home

I am here to say that I Love you. You are a bright star shining in the heavens. We Love each other, forevermore. That is a saying that has Truth within the heart of it. Love is a matter of *Be*-ing — being in the moment, fully. That is, we are *Be*-ing ourselves so deep within, that nothing disturbs our way of *Be*-ing.

Love is armor. It is an invisible shield that protects us from all who seek to disturb our way of *Be*-ing. If only we realized this ever-present Love protects us and keeps us from harm, we would live lives filled with Loving blessings. Instead, we come to this place thinking that our hope for the future is to *attain* Love. That is, we think that we do not have it now, in the present. We believe that we must *do* something to deserve the Love of another. That is not so. Instead, we hold onto these thoughts that permeate our shield of Love, almost creating holes in our energy field.

What we believe can dilute what we truly are. We are Oneness. That is, Love. Love abounds wherever and whenever we are unless we sabotage it by our feelings of fear and loss. We sometimes feel that Love is absent from our lives. No greater unTruth was ever spoken, for Love exists everywhere. It is a force *of* life and *beyond* this life. It is a warming energy that touches us deep within, as well as spreading far beyond our depths.

We have constricted our hearts in this society. That is why we do not feel Love. We hold it confined. We are afraid to feel it from others. It is fear that has replaced free-flowing Love. Our hearts are open to Love. We embrace the Love of others. As a world community we have an opportunity to reach out wide and far to all who wish to join us in Love *Be*-ing.

So be it.

Ramón

If only we remembered
who and what
we Are
every moment,
we would only
express Love.

2/23/01   at home

There is within us a heart of gold. I say that, believing that what we hold most precious is within our heart. We claim that all others have the heart of gold, too. It is golden Light beaming forth from within ourselves. We know that Love is our center-most thought pattern. By that I mean, that we *are* Love and that permeates all of us, our thoughts as well as our feelings.

It is true that we think thoughts that are sometimes not labeled as "Love." But since we *are* Love, *all* that we are is Love, too. We sometimes forget that Love permeates all that we *are* and all that we *do*. We forget, and attempt to transform our Love into some other expression. If only we remembered *who* and *what* we are at every moment, we would only express Love.

It is the mind which can transform our thoughts by not thinking thoughts other than those that are Love-expressed. We can observe the thoughts that float into our awareness. We can tell those thoughts that they are not welcome in our minds. By this action we can free our minds of constant thoughts, thoughts that distress us or express anger or sadness. We can free our minds of cyclical thoughts that keep going round and round in our minds.

How?

By quieting ourselves down and becoming aware of the thoughts that occupy our minds. There is a place of quiet and solitude within our minds where no thoughts disturb us. We can go into that space and be quiet, without thought. It is there that we will find solace, knowing our deepest Self is quiet, original *Be*-ing. Thoughts only exist within the mind. They are not floating around boundlessly.

Our hearts generate the *knowing*, not the *thinking*. We *know* without thought. That is, thought is not necessary to *know*. We come to the end of this dissertation *knowing* without *thinking*. It is in the quiet that we can be aware that we *know*. Words become a way of conveying our knowledge. We say, therefore, "I know that I am an expression of Love. It is the deepest part of me.. I am Love and it is I."

So be it.

Raymian

*Our hearts
generate the "knowing,"
not the "thinking."
We Know
without thought.*

2/25/01 at home

I am waiting for your intention. It is that we continue at a much more rapid pace than we have been corresponding.

Let me know who is telling me this?

I am Raymian.

I, too, would like to move forward more quickly.

Let us begin.

I am here to say that we are One. That is known to both of us. We are part of the same Oneness that permeates *All That Is*; therefore, we *are* One. It is an aspect of that Oneness that we each *are*. We separate our energies into form and Spirit which can communicate with each other through experience. It is knowing that is what we are doing, that is a mystery to many.

We are in a way "talking to ourselves." It is better than feeling that you are alone. We dialog with ourselves all the time. Our voices are heard within, telling us about our feelings and thoughts on various points, issues or persons. We listen to that talk all the time.

Our message to the world is to quiet that incessant talking. It gets in the way of knowing what *is*. We are influenced by what we hear. We also put our attention on the constant chatter. To stop the chatter is a first step in putting our minds at ease. We are forever engaged in dialog. We must discern what we will listen to.

Our hearts are open to Love. Our minds are busy recycling thoughts and feelings to such an extent that the Love in our hearts is clouded by our thoughts and feelings. Another way to say this is that we must choose to pay attention to that which will bring us peace and harmony instead of allowing our thoughts and feelings to dominate our lives.

Our hope is to cry out with Loving thoughts and feelings instead of being dominated by fears and conflicts that we try to resolve. How does this happen? It happens through controlling our own attention. By that I mean, we pay attention only to those thoughts and feelings that we choose.

When thoughts arise we can decide that we do not want to pay attention to them. We tell them or allow them to go away. We intend to focus our minds and hearts on peace and harmony. We are then open to Loving thoughts and feelings. If we take up all our time musing with non-Loving thoughts and feelings, we have stayed with those thoughts and feelings and, therefore, are not truly open to expansive growing, nurturing thoughts and feelings.

Our hope is for Love, that permeates all, to be known to us every moment of every day that we live. It is a hope that is shared by all who come into this life.

So be it.

Raymian

To stop the chatter
is a first step
in putting our minds
at ease.

2/28/01   at home

"Raymian," my name, is Love that has shone forth, beamed forth in Loving-kindness. We are here to Love each other.

I was not afraid when I died to the world you know. Instead, I welcomed the Light.

It is difficult to decide what you are to do every day of the years on Earth. Be guided by Love in everything that you do.

So be it.

And now, I come to say that you are worried about your friend. She is where she is. We never know where we will be. It is a trick of life to face many circumstances. This is one of them. You should know that life is cyclical. We all have times that are active, and other times that are solitary. This is one for her. Decisions will be made through this period. Be not afraid to participate.

Our work will proceed as you wish. We will move more quickly. This episode has shown you that if there is something you wish to accomplish, you must make an effort to do so. Time is not infinite on Earth. We just pass through. When I was there with you, our time was short. But, oh, what we accomplished! We Loved our family and friends. We nurtured our garden of Love. We came into this life to prosper. We lived our lives fully.

Now you ask, "What would make my life full of Love?" That is a different question than you asked earlier in life. We know now that Love is all-important.

You still want to accomplish something. It is so that Love can spread more than it has today. To spread the word of God is a noble pursuit. You have lived fully. You may continue to do so. That is the way to spread Love more fully.

So be it.

Raymian

3/2/01   at home

For all the Love that exists, I am one who *knows* that is what I am.

So be it.

We are One with each other. That is so. Tonight we will speak about caring. "We care," we say. What does that mean? We look after those who are near and dear to us. That is, we cover our sorrows with loving thoughts. We are touched by others' dilemmas when we view them. If we do not turn away, we say we "care." Caring in a way is sharing our Love. We cannot say that we care and not be touched by our own feelings deep within.

We care when the doorbell rings. It is a friend who has come to visit us, one who is willing to share her Self with us. As we are alone too much, is not a stranger better than not knowing someone deeply? By that I mean, we care for the Love that binds us together. We nurture our friendships. We say we care about each other. We do care. Our thoughts are with our Loved ones. That includes our friends.

So be it.

And now, I am leaving for awhile. I have come to honor our time together. It has been for us a parting of ways that stayed on the same path; one in your world and one in mine. I am coming again soon. But this departure is necessary so that I may learn the next steps. You have been impatient sometimes, but now you must wait for me to return renewed. We all have times of solitude and learning and this is such a time for me. Be mindful of the friendship and Love that we share.

So be it.

Ramón

I *be* it. That is, I *know* that which I convey. You *are* Love. That is all there is.

So be it.

And now, in the name of the Father and the Son and the Holy Ghost, I give you Raymian, another aspect of *All That Is*.

Armand

Good evening. I am Raymian, the Love of your lifetime. It is good to be here with you. We have spoken of Love and caring. Now, let us talk of rewards. We each seek something in return for our actions. Let it be known that whatever the result, it is favorable to us. By that I mean, we learn from everything that comes our way. Be not afraid to try something that you have not tried before. As a matter of fact, I do believe that you enjoy trying the new. This is a switch for you. You had been enmeshed in fear. It held you back. But now you try. It is fun and adventurous!

Raymian

*We learn
from everything
that comes our way.*

3/6/01 *flying from Chicago to White Plains*

It is for us a new way of *Be*-ing together. We gather our forces to weld our hopes and dreams. We seek knowledge, forevermore. But it is our hope of a new future that keeps us moving along the path. We think that tomorrow will be better. It will be exciting and welcoming. We know that new challenges await us. We hope that these challenges will offer a means of growth. That is our hope; that we will meet these challenges with grace and enlightenment. So be it.

You ask about our relationship with two of our closest friends. We welcomed our visits to their home. We found Love expressed in ways that made each person feel special. How could a couple find the time and energy to share their lives with so many others? This relationship was special to me. I enjoyed the time we spent together as two families joined as one. We toured historic sites that I probably would never have gone to on my own. It opened another world, a world where families shared their time together. Each person gained something new from the trips.

I never realized how much I cared about the sharing of Love. It was not easy to forfeit the times together when I left. I remember that you went to visit our friends the first Thanksgiving after I died. Our friend kept saying that she felt my presence. I *was* there, sharing your time together! It was a thoughtful episode that brought you all comfort, for you experienced the holiday in a different venue. It brought solace to the heartfelt loss that you were experiencing at the time. I am amazed that you all found yourselves enjoying the encounter. We were alone no more for we had friends that opened their hearts to you.

Part Four

The Heart of the Matter

It is an internal way of Be-ing
so that no matter what you do,
it is from the Source,
from the Heart.

3/11/01   *at home*

I am here waiting for your call. We have much to say today. Our Love is forever. We cannot fathom that anything lasts forever except Love. That is the only thing that continues on forever. It is filled with hopes and dreams eternal.

Our hearts are open to this everlasting Love. It springs forth from within us. It is our Source, the only Source of *all things*. "Things" are not the material items in this sense. In other words, there is nothing that describes Love. We take the vernacular to express ourselves, even though it is not exactly true. "Things" are the possessions that we bear through lifetimes. And yet, in the sense that we are now talking, "things" are nothings, *no-things*. They are merely expressions of Love.

We come into this life with no thing except our growing body. This we leave behind when our time on Earth is over. We express ourselves through this thing, our body, but we do not identify our eternal Souls with it. Instead we are without form and without "things." That is so, no matter how many times we come to Earth for Earthly experience.

And now, I bring you one who is waiting to hear your voice. It is Love of another sort. You were together in life, but are now separated in death. That is, you cannot *see* each other in form.

I am one who knows that you are embarking on a road to salvation. That is, you seek to come to the end of your lifetime reborn into new ways of *Be*-ing.

We each have the capacity to grow, to try out new identities. We think that we have to be literally "born" again to do this. That is not so. We reinvent our Selves through the roles we play on the stage of life. You have been daughter, wife, mother, Lover, artist, writer, magician, and so many other roles. You are now preparing a change of role.

You will soon be leaving your present employed position. It will be traumatic in the sense that it is a great change in life not to be involved with the everyday concerns of the job. That means that you will be free to spend time in other quarters. By that I mean, you shall move onto other "things." It is not meant to say that you will not be busy, for you shall always find ways to occupy your time. You shall know other ways of *Be*-ing, as well as other roles to play.

We have known for a long time that Love is sublime. Now it is time to express this more fully, not only in your lifetime, but also for all lifetimes. By that I mean, we must know from whence we come in order to proceed to the next level of greatness.

We are from the same Source. We know that. We come to tell you that Love is divine, for that is the way to dwell in the hearts of all who come forth to this present day. We know that Love is supreme. That is, there is nothing that is greater than Love.

So be it.

Our tome is about to be finished in a new way. We are no longer going to dwell on past relationships. We shall seek instead to dwell in the heart of the matter. That is, we shall come forth with Love that is suitable to the present moment. By that I mean, we shape our thoughts to the coming forth of Love in a newness that we have not experienced before. It is Love that permeates all things. It is Love that knows what *is*. It is Love that joins the hearts of all who are coming to this realization. We *know*. We *Love*. That is all.

We know Love is supreme. We sometimes act as if Love doesn't exist at all. It is for us to concentrate our efforts on the existence of Loving thoughts and expressions. We *know*. It is so.

So be it.

We have many ideas about the ways to go forth. We are gently prodding you. Be not afraid to take on new ways. It shall be enlightening, so to say!

You question, "What are these new ways?" They are ways of Loving other beings. We cannot help those who cannot sense that they are of the Light Beings. We need help to access their hearts. It is through stories such as those of you and Raymian that we will be able to connect more fully. It is important that the two of you complete your present work together so that it can be published. There are many who seek communication with those whom they have known on Earth, those whom they trusted on an intimate level. This is a necessary step in our process of bringing to Light new ways of *Be*-ing.

You have been using this form of communication for many years. It is the thoughts and transmissions that must come to light. It is saying that the sources available to us have expanded beyond our own cognition. We are information sharers from another Internet, the Celestial Web! Be not afraid to share the access domain with all who seek to "log on!"

And now, I will tell you of Love and glory that awaits all who tune in. We are here, accessible to the heart. We have waited for a long time to open our website to any and all who seek to share and chat with us. You are now used to the localized Earth network. Please connect to the Celestial Web, for you shall find Joy and sharing beyond your dreams!

It is tuning time for all who wish to raise their level of awareness. It shall be Oneness that we seek through joining our forces, our Love and Light forces.

And now is the time for all to join our hearts' own dream to be One with *All That Is*. This is a way to Truth and Light, to Love and life fulfilled with new blessings.

So be it.

And now, I hope you are energized by all there is to be!

Raymian

*We are
information sharers
from another Internet,
the Celestial Web!*

3/17/01 at home

This morning you came to me while I was still in bed. Will you repeat what you said so that I can record it here?

I am waiting for you to help me with our lesson for today. It is so that I can be one with you. We know what is in our hearts. We shall know that our Love for each other on Earth lingers in the hearts of all those we have known. That is, it stays with them as they remember something that we said or did, or just that we were with them.

Our hearts record our loving moments. We know when someone is sending us loving thoughts and energy. The record remains, ever to tap as a source of inspiration. That is how we inspire others, through their hearts' memory.

Sometimes we quote another. The words are empty without the loving energy behind the thoughts. When we are inspired, our heart's energy grows from the flame ignited by those words, acts or deeds. We inspire others with our loving thoughts, deeds and acts.

You notice that I use both the words "act" and "deed." Our action may be just to *Be* in the moment with the other person. We may not *do* anything. We must make that distinction for only the visible acts and/or deeds are recognized in your world. We must know that there is more to action than the doing. It is the heart of the matter that propels one forward with inspired deeds.

And now, I bring you one who is waiting to tell you of Love from another source. By that I mean, we are in ourselves sources of the Source. So when I refer to an individualized person or other entity, I sometimes refer to that individualization as "source."

It is true that we are beings from another plane. There are many so-called planes or dimensions. I am in a realm of Light that is conveyed to you via your heart. You hear me internally. You are not using your ears, so to say. Instead, you are hearing me from a source that exists other than your individualized Spirit.

You can access others and me by quieting the thoughts and asking that we communicate with you. It is so that we can benefit from each other's experiences. You are on Earth, experiencing life as a woman — daughter and mother. It is so that you will know once again what it is like to make decisions that affect the lives of others, as well as contribute to your growth and well-being.

We are here on Earth as visitors who come to assist you in your endeavors. It is not to interfere, but rather to guide you in the decisions you make. It is not that we are smarter than you, but that we are focused on the Love that differentiates your way of *Be*-ing from ours.

We know that Love is the Source of *All That Is*. We focus our energies on contributing our actions to your knowing, or realizing that life spent coming from the heart is very different than life spent without this focus. You can live "successfully" by your deeds. You are taught to hold onto goals and accomplish them. We here have but one goal: to *be* Love in its many manifestations.

We are not saying that you should not accomplish anything or that goals are unnecessary. We only say that Love must be at the heart of the matter. That is, all deeds are measured by their ability to Love while accomplishing the task.

We know that this might not make complete sense to you. You have been taught to Love one another. How can you do your "work" while you focus on Loving one another? It is not an external focus on "Loving" the other person. It is an internal way of *Be*-ing so that no matter what you do, it is from the Source, from the heart.

When you have decisions to make, do you ask yourself whether this is coming from the heart? Do you seek ways of *Be*-ing with others that show that you have peaceful thoughts? Do you share the Loving energy you feel inside with those you meet by "just being yourself?" By that I mean, your true Love-based Self that shows without any effort. I mean that Love is not necessarily a demonstrable action viewed as movement. It is just there, permeating all that is also there. When you are in a peaceful Loving state it is evident to those you meet without your doing or saying anything.

And now, I know that you must go to prepare a place to work. It is for you a blessing to be able to work from your home. You have spent almost twenty years commuting to and fro for four to five hours each day. To be relieved of that strain is a blessing. You will be able to concentrate more fully on your work and on our work. It is a transition from one type of focus to another. Be not afraid to enjoy every benefit that relays to you.

And now, I give you Raymian, who is patiently waiting for a

word with you.

You know that we are developing a new way of *Be*-ing between our worlds. It is not difficult in the sense that we have worked together before. The difficulty arises in our saying all that we need to say to each other in a way that others may benefit from our experience.

Our hearts are joined in Love. We know what it is to be One on Earth, as well as through this communication. It is not that the relationship as husband and wife continues. It is that two Souls joined once on Earth are never separated thereafter; for a "piece" of each's energy is mingled with the other's and cannot be separated once it is totally assimilated.

You are who you are partly because we spent sixteen years together. We grow from every experience, like the plant that is watered by the rainstorm and takes minerals from the Earth where it is planted. Those elements become part of the plant forevermore and cannot be separated or cleansed from the plant's body in such a way that the original Source can be identified. We are *always* part of one another.

We shall separate our individualized Spirits, but we can recall the experience of the lifetime we shared. We need not dwell on that experience as we proceed to new ways of *Be*-ing and relating. We can recall at will, and we can choose not to recall, as well.

It is the choice that is important to our well-being. We can dwell in the past circumstance, or we can move on. Our hearts can help us find new ways of expressing Love. We need not dwell in the heart of the matter that we experienced in the past. We can move onto new experiences that challenge our senses, that grow our Spirit and that bring Joy and hope to all those who we touch. It is a matter of heart leading the way.

And now, I bring you Love in the highest. To know the Source of *All That Is* is the highest level of *Be*-ing. Be One with *All That Is* and you shall prosper in your heart of hearts.

So be it.

I Love you deeply in the sense that we are One, now and forevermore.

Raymian

*. . . life spent
coming from the heart
is very different
than life spent
without this focus.*

3/18/01 at home

I am here to Love one that is *All That Is.* By that I mean, we are all Oneness. It permeates all there is.

I am here to settle your heart's strings. By that I mean, we each come to a place where we must make decisions that will affect our lives thereafter. Yours is in limbo because you are turning from one set of ways to another. You have been focusing on the job and your inner work. Time has come to get organized in a new direction! You have much to do. It will be easier if you have arranged things so that the flow is uninterrupted. By that I mean, we each have items that direct our lives. It is for you a time to rid yourself of the items from which you have been detached but have not let go. Go forth with a clean slate, so to say!

You are right. All that I have accumulated keeps me from moving forward with ease. It is a burden to carry all this stuff with me.

Our hearts are joined in loving-kindness. We know that those we encounter are also making their way through this world. Our hope is to find Joy that eludes our every waking hour. It is there of course, but we do not perceive that it is there.

And now, I convert the lesson to one of loneliness that has found an inner Source of peace and comfort. We each elude ``loneliness'' in a different way. Some seek out new adventures, stimulation that makes them forget that they are lonely. Others seek company to assuage the throes of a lonely nature.

You do neither for this reason. You are not lonely in the sense of which I am speaking. Your comfort comes from within. It does not exude peacefulness; it only dispels thoughts of loneliness. We are lonely when we *think* we are lonely. It is a state of mindfulness that can distort the Truth.

We are centered in a realm of beings that communicate with each other. It is like logging on to the Internet. We can find someone online, day or night. That is the way of celestial beings. We are always "up," waiting for your call!

Once in a while we speak with you without waiting for your call. It is necessary to plant ideas sometimes, even though you may not ask for them. Our hope is that you will welcome some input. If not, then you will just deny that anything else occurred to you. It is a message of hope for the future. We are available for communicating. Our hearts are bound to yours. We will communicate with you or will remain silent, as you wish.

Today is a bright and sunny day. It is approaching the Equinox, a time of equal day and night. Seldom do we find our world in such balance. More often day and night are of unequal length. It is unnecessary to vary the day's routine when Light shines more fully in our hearts. When we are aware of the fullness of *Be*-ing, we are indeed helpful, unpressured and living *in* and *through* this fullness. Be not afraid to exist at this level of *Be*-ing. One who is filled with Light, Love and Joy is indeed fulfilled.

So be it.

We are coming to the end of this lesson. It is a pleasure to speak with you. Now, in the name of all that is, I give you Raymian.

We are Oneness. That is the lesson for today. It is repeated here because we are telling it in such a way that all can understand. Our hearts are whole. That is, we are not separate in all that we do. Instead, we are One. It is a lesson that is difficult to fathom for we are taught otherwise. It is a new day that requires that we think in new ways.

So be it.

And now, I bring you greetings of Love and Light from all who are bound to the Earth by experiences thereon.

We dwell in the Light. Dark forces are unknown here. Be in the Light and you shall shine so brightly that you will know of which I speak.

Raymian

It is a new day
that requires
that we think
in new ways.

3/20/01 at home

This is an exciting time, for I am beginning to telecommute after nineteen years of commuting four and a half to five hours a day. I feel so relieved of the burden of traveling so far every day. I chose to go to New York City so our daughters could stay here in the home and community where they grew up. We had a community network that I could depend upon and who would look out for the girls.

It was a hard decision to go to New York. Part of it was the pay. I couldn't find anything else in this area that came close to the opportunities that the job in NYC offered. I have no doubt that I was meant to make the contributions that I did.

Now I am about to embark on a new road, one that is filled with trepidation and, at the same time, knowing that it will be all right. I have an inkling of life after New York. It will be quieter, filled with hope and dreams.

One thing that occurred to me a long time ago is that everyday is like every other day; every year is like every other year. By that I mean, we are always looking forward to the next step, no matter what it is. There is always a next step; we just don't know where it will lead.

Our hearts are open to newness as we contemplate the next step. You have been cleaning out residue from the past. It is time to finish that job for now and to plan your place for the future. Ways will be different as we move on.

And now, I bring you one who is waiting to converse.

It is I, the one and only one, who knows your thoughts and deeds. We are separated only by the veil of Light between worlds. Our hope is to be One with each other. I am a part of you that seeks to come out into the Light. Help your Self to know the ways of Light beings. Our hearts' desire is to Love our Self, as much as, if not even more than anyone else.

(I fell asleep!)

3/21/01   at home

We are here to bless the Earth with Loving-ness. We have come to say that you are trying too much. Ever since you started working at home, you have been on the move. It is not like you to keep constantly going. It is better to keep in touch with your innermost being as you adjust to a new way of *Be*-ing. This not to say that you have wandered off the path, but rather that you have not found a way to feel rested as you do so much. It will come.

Our hearts are bound not by circumstances but by Love deep within us. We know that we are commuting between worlds. There is no place to drive, walk, or take a train. You may stay in one place or move along your path. We will be with you no matter where you are. There is no need to set up fancy conditions to ritualize our communication. There is no need to have quiet surroundings. There is only focusing your intention on this communication no matter where you are or what you are doing.

Some people need quiet to listen to their Selves. But we engage in constant chatter, no matter where we are or what we are doing. The force of internal chatter that comes from previous experiences can drown out the voice of the true Self, as well as communications from other dimensions.

I am calling from "the other side." It is done without wires and without headsets. We have a built-in mechanism for communication. We have just used only a small part of it. We shall continue to learn more ways of communicating with ourselves, as well as with others.

Our bond in life was strong enough to make it easy to communicate between worlds. It is not always so, for some desire to communicate but are not sure that this is possible. When they hear a voice from beyond the veil, they dismiss it as something they may have made-up. It is not easy to believe that we are not inventing this whole communication system.

For you, it took many years to become comfortable with this form of communication. You had glimpses of it as a youngster. Periodically, something would pop into your head; a profound thought or message would come to you. Some of those messages you remember to this very day. You will never forget the Truth. It stays with you.

It is now time to put your thoughts and messages to work. By that I mean, you have known for a long long time that you were to be a teacher. It is through communications such as this that the message line between the two worlds will develop into a true celestial network.

You have known for a long time that you are one of many who will join this work. It is not really work, so playfully attend to it! By that I mean, we must remember how to communicate beyond this world. It is not difficult, nor is it a struggle. Instead it is a blessing. Be Joyful in your work. In that way it shall be like playing rather than working.

Our hearts are bound together. We are not separate. We Love what we do. It is a sacred journey and we must enjoy it, for it does indeed bring Joy to our mindfulness. We must be careful with words that can be misunderstood. Joy exists more fully within each of us than we are aware. When we know that basic Truth that in our center is Joy, we shall be Joyous. We are not currently Joyous because we have digressed from the knowledge of our own Source of Joy. To know one's Self more fully is to know the Joy of all lifetimes combined into one.

Raymian

There is no need
to set up fancy
conditions
to ritualize
our communication.

3/23/01   at home

I am waiting to communicate with you. Our hearts are joined in knowing that Love is *All That Is*. It is seldom said that our Joy is fullness personified. That is because we are always communicating lack. We cannot be in our fullness if we are preoccupied by *lack* of fullness. Whenever we fill our hearts with Joy, we know that of which I speak. Seldom do we experience that fullness. We are craving something that we think we don't already have. It is that lack that drives our fullness away.

Just think of what it would be like to experience Joy in our every waking moment. It would be bliss in the highest sense. Then, why not experience Joy? Because we think that we need something more than what we currently have to bring on this feeling of fullness. We deceive ourselves, for we need nothing more than our own Self.

Our hearts are tranquil. It is sensing our own *Be*-ing that brings about that state of tranquility. Our hearts are our domains. By that I mean, we dwell in the Joy of Truth with thanksgiving for the expression of Joyous fulfillment.

So be it.

And now, I bring you Raymian to guide the conversation toward those matters of importance. By "matters of *import*ance" I mean that we think Love is something external; that it is something that must be *drawn* to us. Our hearts are opened to this external Love only to be disappointed that another's Love does not fill us with perpetual Joy.

It is true that we have choices to make. We choose to know our Selves better each day. It is a foible that we are knowledgeable for we say, "Our hearts are full," only to experience loneliness. A lack of Spirit tends to manifest as loneliness. We are sure that this feeling of loneliness will soon depart. It takes but a moment of knowing that our hearts are at the center of our universe to say, "I Love you."

And now, I bid you adieu.

Raymian

3/24/01 at home

Our hearts are welcoming you to our fold. It is not that we are separate but that we have been seperated for a long time. That is that we are always here, but unaware of each other. Our hearts are dwelling in a mire of circumstances that cloud our thoughts and make it difficult to proceed with our communication.

Our hearts are centers of Light. That is, we are brightness *within*. Some seek the Light *without*. It is true that it is there, for Light is everywhere. But our hearts are our own Source of Light.

I remember you sought Light within, but could not see it. During meditation someone would say, "See the point of light within growing brighter."

I could not see it when I forced myself to focus on an illusory point of light.

But it is there, nonetheless. For we *are* Light within, shrouded by our Earthly bodies. Sometimes the body hides the Light because we have drawn it secretly within our Selves. We make decisions that hamper our free-flowing waves of Light. We decide to keep what we have all to ourselves. Call it "self-preservation," call it "helplessness" or call it "fear." These are all acts of withholding Love from one another.

We dwell in the hearts of all those we meet. We know we are connected, for we *are* Oneness. And yet we forget to share our Light with all those we meet.

You have been experiencing the power of the smile. That is recognition of the Light in others. To smile is to connect our beings. It is beautiful to see the Light of others come to the surface from deep within. Smiles born of Love are catching! People who you do not know, so-called "strangers," respond to the call of Love that penetrates deep into the seat of their Souls. It is true that we are each Sources of Light and Love.

Go Be it!

Raymian

*Smiles
born of Love
are catching!*

3/28/01 at *Pizzeria*

I just looked at my watch and realized that today would have been Ray's sixty-ninth Birthday. I've been going through some old boxes and found an Easter card from Ray to his father written when he was a little boy. Do you remember that card?

I do. It was an attempt to assuage my feelings about the absence of my father. He was always away working. We lived in New Paltz later on, but that was to be closer to Dad. He was a chef who worked at a resort. He lived and worked there.

And now, I will tell you how much I Loved you. You were the light of my life. I had tried to escape poverty when I was young, but to no avail. It wasn't until our conversation about my self-image as a poor boy that I was able to put those thoughts away forever. You said that no one knows where we come from. We only know what is on the surface right now. That is, unless someone has told us something about past history.

We each carry our own stories with us. It is out of that scenario that we act. We believe that the world can see us and all that we have struggled with in the past. After all, we carry those memories within us. Is not that the way that others see us?

"No," you said, "It is only what you share or do that others see." You cannot convey your whole life history to others. You choose what you want them to know about you. You said, "Forget that you were a poor boy and no one else will even have an inkling of it. Demonstrate who you are now, not who you were before."

I did just that. I forgot how poor I had been. Instead, I thought, "How lucky we are to have all that we have. We want for nothing." It is easy to cloud the present situation with thoughts of bygone days. That was what I was doing: remembering how I was taunted and otherwise ill-treated when we lived in a house that only had a dirt floor. We were poor in material goods, but never poor in Spirit.

My mother painted candles for a living. My father cooked. I worked at the boarding house, helping out in the kitchen as well as doing odd jobs. Those were the years when I learned so much about life. I learned to be discerning at the grocery store. I learned how to handle the little money we had. I was the "big man" around the house because my father was away. It taught me responsibility.

I'll never forget the lessons learned working at the boarding house and later in the pharmacy. I wanted to become a pharmacist like the owner. But that was not to be. The only school in town was a teachers' college. So that was what I studied.

You and I were both teachers. That was how we met. The Teacher's Association sponsored a bowling league. I was a really good bowler! I saw you there. We bet on your score. You won, so I had to take you out for dinner. That was the beginning of our relationship on Earth.

We never know how a chance meeting can change the course of our lives. I know that it was meant to be. We knew that it was forever a relationship of the heart.

So be it.

I am coming to tell you that instant recognition is rarely an accident. It is a *knowing* of sorts. I am One with you, now and forever. It is an example of Love traveling through the realms of glory.

Go forth and know that Love is conveyed through our *knowing*. Be not skeptical of *knowing* instantly.

Raymian

It is easy
to cloud
the present situation
with thoughts
of bygone days.

3/30/01   at home

The light is dim today. The clouds hide the sun. That is much like our story of life lived. We only show the bright side occasionally. We sometimes hide behind circumstances that cloud that which we truly *are*.

We come to expect that talk is superficial. It does not reach the depths of the Soul. That is because we are taught to protect ourselves, to play at the superficial level and to disclose very little about our "true" Selves. It is a shame that we do this.

We could use all the energy that we use to hide our Selves to better purpose. We contemplate the most wonderful visions of a world where sharing and supporting of one another is the accepted way. Then, we go from our sacred place of contemplation as if we were a totally different person from the one touched deep within.

And now, I bring you Raymian, the guide of your lifetime to be with you in this new Whole-some way.

It is true that we are of the many Souls that have passed through life on Earth. We have come to be in form, to know the ways of Loving in density. It is our way of knowing that we Love each other more than we can imagine. By that I mean, we come to know that there is within each the Spirit of a Loved one.

And now, I bring you a surprise. It is that we are coming to the mid-point in our exercise of jotting down the words that pass between us. It is for us a lessening of the strain of doing this. It is taxing to try to communicate on many levels at once, so this is practice at that kind of communication. We have established a way that proceeds quickly. Our hearts are cured of the Loving that is missing one another. We know that we are never far from one another.

And now, I bring you loving thoughts of hope for a new way of *Be*-ing. It is to relax a bit more, not be strained by anything that you do. Be One with *All That Is* and you shall be relaxed and *knowing*. That is a way of sages: to know what *is* without trying to control it in any way.

And now, we come to the end of this tome. It is fruitful to continue to communicate for now. We will comply with our promise to tell the world of our letters laid to paper. You can see that our communication has grown slowly but fruitfully.

What was just said doesn't make sense to me. We are at the mid-point and also at the end of this tome. Could you tell me what you mean by this?

It is the end of a chapter. It is not the end of our conversing. We know how little we can convey through the written word. Be not afraid to tell others about what we have written. We will continue. Fear not.

And now, I come with newness of life eternal. We *know*, we *Love* and we *are*.

So be it.

Raymian

That is a way of sages:
to know what Is
without
trying to control it
in any way.

Part Five

A New Way of Be-ing

The secret is Be-ing while Doing!

04/06/01   at home

So what do you think about my cleaning out the house?

It's about time to settle into a new way of life. We change what we do every so often. That helps us to grow and provides excitement in the daily doings. Thinking about something different is helping the Soul to reconnect in a different way. By that I mean, we come to Earth as a baby who has much to learn. As the child grows she leaves behind childish things. So it is with other stages of life. You carry your ability to access old ways but must concentrate on what is new to you. That is growth in a healthy way.

I think that all I left behind is useless in this form. It holds no magical solution to loneliness. Instead it is a burden to those who must dispose of it. By that I mean, it holds no special quality just because I used it in a lifetime. Museums are filled with items of those departed. They show what instruments were used during that "time period," nothing else.

I know that I do not miss physical things. What I miss is the blending of energies on an ongoing basis. It must be the same for you. It is the spiritual energy that fills the void left when one departs. Many people can feel the energy pattern of one whom they have known in form. Others think that this is impossible. We each handle it in our own way. For us, we continue to communicate. It is a strengthening of resolve to do this work that keeps our energies blended.

And now, I come to say that I am delighted that you are able to spend more time in your house. It will be an interesting enterprise to see how you convert the home into a studio for welcoming all who wish to share your thoughts and this enterprise. Things will not stay the same. They never do. Our hearts are open to new ways of *Be*-ing.

And now, I bring you the dawning of a new age. By that I mean, we are welcoming a new way of *Be*-ing where we acknowledge our connection to each other. We are separate only in thought that has been molded by our times and customs. You are aware that others do not share the same orientation in which you were schooled at a young age; therefore, there is much to learn from each other.

Our tales shall enlighten the Souls of all who are One with *All That Is*.

So be it.

Raymian

Do we forget
that we have
the Source of Light
within us?

04/12/01   at home, 2:30 a.m.

I know that this is a time of *knowing* what to do. It is also a time of knowing what *not* to do for we are always *doing* or *being*. The secret is *Be*-ing *while* doing. That is, to be in a state of happiness as we go about our daily doings. This state eludes many people. That is why we seek happiness. It is there all the time. It does not disappear; it goes underground, so to say. By that I mean, we cover up our happiness with all kinds of woes.

We are forever seeking to kindle the flame of happiness. There is no need to do so. Happiness is more like the old-fashion pilot light. It glows incessantly. One cannot shut off the old pilot light and still have a flame that will light other flames as it is called upon. We kindle our Spirit from a spark that is forever Lighting the way. We need not seek other sources of happiness. We possess all there is *within* us.

Enough said about kindling the Spirit. Our hearts are open to new ways of *Be*-ing. We call upon our inner resources as we go about our daily business. We have an unlimited Source of Light. We access it through the heart portal. We know what it is to Love one another. That is a sharing of the Light within each of us.

Our heart is open to a new Light. We suppose that Light exists everywhere. That is so. The darkness seems a void but it, too, has Light hidden in its depths. So it is with each of us. We hide the Light that is there. Are we afraid to access our own inner being? Do we forget that we have the Source of Light *within* us? Are we afraid that we will lose whatever Light we are generating if we share that Light with others?

Whatever we *think* imposes its limitations on the heart's core being. It is our thoughts that can transform our way of *Be*-ing. Think not of the darkness. Think only of Light. Access your being through thoughts of Loving-kindness. To serve another, one must access this deep resource to blend Loving energies with *All That Is*.

We know that smiles are a sign of Loving-kindness. We blend our hopes for another person with our own inner being when we smile. It is for us an act of Love. To see someone, who is unknown to us, smile is for us a great gift of Love.

Our hearts are forever telling us of new Light that shines forth through our *Be*-ing. It fills every void. It holds hope and promise for a new day. We need only allow that day to fill our hearts overwhelmingly. It is True that we are ones who can *be* One.

So be it.

And now, I bring you loving hope and kindness, forevermore.

Raymian

We cannot expect
our way
to be the way
of others.

4/13/01 at home, 3:30 a.m.

It is welcoming that you are awake at this time. We are awaiting your call. It is time to begin our dialog. We will talk about what is to come. Our hearts are open to all kinds of things. That is, we welcome the newly demonstrated ways of *Be*-ing. Our hearts are known for the Love that resides within. It is for us to allow the Love that we have to go forth from our Source.

This is easier said than done in a world filled with strife.

And now, our hearts are open to the dawning of the new day. Look outside and you will see darkness. That is only temporary.

Later that day

We are *Be*-ing. That is, we have the capacity to *be* what we *are*. We seldom practice all that we can be. Instead, we are focused on little things. The major life experiences are those that transform our life, which bring us closer to our Source of Love. Love is at the heart of matter.

So be it.

You are entering on a new lifetime of Love and forgiving-ness. We are bound with our hopes and dreams. Your dream is to be useful in spreading the Truth. It is what we all know deep down inside. There are many paths to the Truth. All shall lead to the Truth. We cannot expect our way to be the way of others. Each must find his own way.

Experiences open the senses to new ways of perceiving the "real" world. Beyond those senses is another level of *knowing*. When we encounter the Truth, we *know* it. Our role is to discover the Truth that lies hidden in all those experiences. How we handle what happens to us, changes as we progress toward the Truth. You and I know moments of discovery in the little things that we do. Remember the Light that shines within whenever and wherever you are.

So be it.

We have not spoken about the fact that we did not discuss the possibility of doing the work that we are now engaged in when I was with you on Earth. It was the furthest thing from my mind. Our spiritual paths were a given. We did not need to discuss our beliefs. That is why it came as somewhat of a surprise that we should engage in this dialog. Our hearts were bound on Earth but life was too short to even contemplate death. It was not in my thinking.

We went on from day to day, doing the things that all people do when they are fully engaged in life, or so it seems. Our voices were not turned to the thought of death. It came as suddenly and yet as gently as a knock on the door. I did not realize what was happening until it was over. What a shock to be there one moment and gone the next!

You had to turn your life around from being a homemaker and volunteer to be the "bread winner." We often have life-altering experiences. Perhaps not of this level, but the potential for change is always there. You had to reinvent yourself. In those days "Dress For Success" was very important. You clothed yourself in business attire. It was fun, anxiety building and successful. Whether you would have to do that today is another story! The clothes transformed the outer you, but deep inside you were firm in your convictions to do whatever was necessary to provide for our children.

Today you face another life-altering decision. It is to do this work in such a way that others can benefit from it. There is no doubt that it will be life altering. I say that because you will be called upon to explain what we are doing. Those who know will not ask. Those who do not know how to access the "other side" will want to know. Or better yet, will want to try!

There will be confrontation from those who are of different persuasions. That is what you have been preparing for. All the various opinions cannot deter you from sharing this work. I am here to support you. It is difficult not to be there in body, but someone else will step forward and play that role. We are each alone, and yet, not *apart*.

You have stuck with your resolve in doing what you could for our daughters. Now it is time to shift to the greater world in sharing this manuscript. We all know that we will be called upon to do that which we were intended to do. We now see that we do that over and over again.

So be it.

I look forward to this challenge!

We shall not weaken our promises. We shall indeed proceed.

Raymian and *Denice*

We are alone
in our views,
but
we are not alone.

4/17/01   *Akron, Ohio*

I know that you are hesitant to contact me while you are away from home. Our Love permeates all time and distance. We know that our Love will continue to bind us to one another as we proceed with our daily activities, no matter where we are.

Our heads and hearts can be in two places at once. Sometimes that is an unsettling experience! We try to keep focused with brainpower and our heart's Loving energy coordinated, or shall I say focused, on the same thing. When you are "out of town," it means that you have left one area to be in another. But not all of you has taken the step to go elsewhere. Instead, a bit of you is left behind, for you continue to live at the same address. People send or direct their energy to your place of business or abode. It is as if you were there, but you are not.

You've left a message in the message box telling people that you will call them. It is as if there were an alter ego reclining in the wings, waiting for her turn to perform on stage. Imagine leaving your print, voiceprint, for others to identify when they wish to contact you! Who are you? Are you flesh and blood sitting at a computer pouring forth this missive? Are you the voice behind the message box? Are you neither of these? Who are you? How can you be in two places at once?

First, listen to the voice of Love flowing forth. It comes to tell you that Love lasts longer than any other emotion. It is well worth putting your efforts behind all that you do, for Love is all there is!

Raymian

4/19/01 *flying from Chicago to White Plains*

I am wondering whether we can continue with the last message?

You know, Denice, that *All There Is* **is** Love and Light. That is energy shared with force and the power of Love. It is nothing else. We encapsulate our own loving energy as we go forth to other places. We know how to share *All That Is* with all there is otherwise. By that I mean, that we discern what *is* and what *is not*, sort of the same question as "To be or not to be?"

There appears to be more than one way to look at things. We *see* what we don't see. We *hear* what we don't hear. We tell tales that are formulated through our own lens. Two people see a situation differently and tell two different tales. We have come to depend on others to validate our views. How can they say "it is so," when they see it differently? If they see it differently, how can they validate our views?

We are alone in our views, but we are not *alone*. We are interrelated in a way that can be described as Oneness. We *are* One. When we remember that we *are* One, and that Truth is the basis of our existence, there is no need for validation. For there is One Truth that is shared by all at the center of their being.

Our hope is to access this Truth in our every waking moment so that we can conduct ourselves in such a way as to epitomize that which we *know*.

So be it.

Rymian

Our forgiveness
is life-giving,
both
to ourselves
and
to those
who annoy us.

04/22/01   at home

I know that you are wondering why the last dialogs were so choppy. It is because you were under strain from illness and the work that you had to do. All is well. We will go forward from here.

Our hearts are open to new ways of *Be*-ing. That is, we want to know more about living *in the moment* all of the time. Our hearts are crying out for peaceful understanding when we engage others in such a way that stress results. We are peaceful beings. That is our natural way. We flow through life taking in the scenery, so to say. We test ourselves with new experiences, and we try not to repeat those experiences that upset our peacefulness. That is easier said than done! What we must remember is that we have in our hearts an overwhelming Love and peacefulness. It permeates *All That Is*, if we will let it.

When we are upset, we must seek to find the inner strength that lies in the heart of Love, the deep well of forgiveness that we apply to those around us and to ourselves. Our forgiveness is life-giving, both to ourselves and to those who annoy us. We can shower our beams of life-giving Light and Love on those who upset our way of *Be*-ing. By that I mean, we Love ourselves so much that nothing can permeate our peacefulness. That is an ideal way of handling whatever situation we might face. Our own inner being has the ammunition of Love to shine forth. Those whom we perceive as attacking us receive from us all that there is to give. It blends with their energy and melts away the negativity. Seldom do we stop to think that we have this strength within us. We revolt with like-action instead of drawing upon the power *within*.

We can create a new way of *Be*-ing from our inner Sources. We have forgotten that this "new way" is not new. We have always possessed this inner strength of *Be*-ing. We just forgot that it is there. To rediscover our own inner being is like the Light that dispels the darkness as the sun rises on a new day, lighting the night skies. Each day brings new light, and yet that light was always there. It was hidden by a turn of events, by the turning of the Earth away from its source of light. A new day, a new way of *Be*-ing, is not new, only another opportunity to begin again each and every moment on Earth. How fortunate we are that we get to choose how we will live each and every moment!

Raymian

Our love of doing
is waning
as we tire of
constantly " doing "
without
" renewing. "

4/25/01   at *Pizzeria*

I have a new deal for you. It is to be a Lover of life-giving forces that are permeating the world today. It is as if a new day was coming upon the Earth. By that I mean, a dawning of a new way of *Be*-ing on Earth. We have been confused by messages of Love that promise newness. Instead, we should see a new way as *Be*-ing in the moment, fully. That way there is no past or future.

Everything that exists, exists *now*. There can be no comparison, for there is nothing to compare "whatever" *to*. We need not waste the *now* by dreaming of times to come, or remembering past experiences. When we are fully here, we *are*. That is, we are *Be*-ing in the moment. Never again shall this moment be, nor shall we be in the moment that has passed. To be in *the now* is to be fully present, no wondering about what is, for it *is*.

We shall know of that which I speak now, not later. Only those who have not arrived in the present will keep looking for it. We *are*, we *shall be*, *now* and forevermore.

So be it.

It is a matter of being aware at every moment that we are, as we have always been told, One with *All That Is*. Our connection is profound. It is one link in the chain of understanding. For we are present with ourselves and with each other, as Oneness is linked with humankind and *All That Is* at once.

It is difficult to ponder such a situation, especially when your focus has been otherwise. We have spent much of our time on Earth choosing one experience over another. We have known that there is another way to be. But this other way requires a shift in the total being's understanding of what *is*. We are not the height of glory. We are not the depths of despair. We are neither the unknown nor the known. We just are what *is*, now and forevermore.

So, "What is?"

What is, is what *is*. Why do we need to ask, "What is?" That is an anomaly. Only one who is not aware asks this question. You are aware. Why do you ask?

I am one who is trying to explain to another how one attains an understanding of what is.

You are trying to come to a conclusion. That is the antithesis of what *is*. We are now in the highest order of knowing what *is*, and yet we deny that we know what *is*.

We are trying to explain what cannot be explained. It must be lived. That is, you will know what *is* as you go about all that you experience. We call to ourselves a series of experiences that will draw a picture of what *is*. That is not possible, but we keep trying! To *try* is to perceive that we are making progress. We are not in the business of making progress, only in *Be*-ing in the situation and maintaining our mode of *Be*-ing.

So be it.

It is for us a way of *Be*-ing in the situation of our choosing. We come to this Earth plane to *be* in the moment. All else that we perceive distracts us. When we try to return to our state of *Be*-ing, we find pressures exerted upon our being that distort our desire. We succumb to the external wants and desires of the "real" world.

Our state of *Be*-ing changes to adjust to those external pressures. We are saluted for our conformity to artificial states of *Be*-ing. We are applauded for our conformity to the social norms. We are accepted into the status of belonging with others "just like us." Are we "really" like those other people or are we different? Is our drummer in tune with the rest of the band? We hope so, for we strive to belong. We adopt the social norms. We praise others who also conform. We are happy to know that we are accepted in this artificial world.

We continue to work toward our goals. We have truly achieved what we have set out to do. Praise be to the Love of achievement for we have reached the heights! Or have we? Are we happy? On the surface, yes! But beneath it all we have a gnawing sensation that feels empty. We have achieved the world, and yet we feel empty. We have done everything that was expected of us, but we feel as if something more important than all that we have achieved is missing.

What could that be? Are we not applauded for all that we have done? Don't we have all that we ever wanted? What is missing? Our sense of belonging is temporarily based on the acceptance of others. Our achievements must continue or else we will be perceived as not doing our share. Our love of *doing* is waning as we tire of constantly doing without renewing. What is wrong with this picture?

It is dependent on external stimuli. It is only driven by inner desire to seek approval and exaltation from others. The more we achieve, the more we need to achieve to keep up. There is a limit to our success.

Meanwhile, we care about our real purpose in life. We seek to find that which will truly bring a sense of satisfaction to us at every moment. What could possibly give us a sense of fulfillment? It is a mystery to us, for we have looked to the world for our adulation. We now know that no matter what others say, we must feel fulfilled ourselves.

We look within where we have that emptiness. How could we possibly fill that cavernous feeling when we have shared ourselves with the world and still feel unfulfilled? We know that we have done everything that we have been told to do, and yet we find no solace in our accomplishments. Could it be that we have looked to others to fulfill our dreams? Could it be that we alone are responsible for our feelings? No one else is to blame for the way that we feel. How could we have lived our lives seeking something that provides us with such emptiness? Could we have been detoured from our original purpose?

No one can answer those questions for you. We each know what we are here to accomplish. The path is different for each of us. In the end though, we shall be fulfilled if we return to our original purpose. To be in the *now* will bring us closer to that goal. So our first step is to be in the *now*, now and forevermore.

So be it.

Raymian

Much of the time
on Earth
we have
forgotten
our origins.

4/26/01   at home

Today is the day that I'm having the electric service to the house upgraded. It has been a long time coming. When we bought this house nearly forty years ago the electric energy being supplied was more than adequate. Today our lives require much more energy.

The connection to the Source must be upgraded so that more energy can be utilized! Perhaps that is so with our lives and our relationship to the Source of our energy? Much has been dependent on a connection that is inadequate for what we want to do with our lives today. We no longer want to rely on our fellowmen to supply our needs. We want a reliable Source that is generated from *within* our being. Of course that Source has always been there, just like the electricity generated by the power company.

What is different is how we tap into the Source. Our wires are too small, frayed and connected through a box that limits the pathways or circuits that we can use. Water has gotten into the system increasing resistance and dropping the voltage available for our use. This is a metaphor for life. Our energy is depleted not by the Source, but by the barriers that we have erected or accumulated as we have lived life.

Today those barriers will be discarded. A new junction will enable us to have a free flowing source of energy entering into our home. So it is with our heart. We have erected barriers and accumulated memories that keep our hearts bound with resistance to opening up the free flow of energy. To discard those accumulations is to open a new pathway to our Source.

4/27/01 at home

I am wondering if the need to communicate varies with the way that I feel? It seems that I cannot access the divine when I am very tired or lack enthusiasm for this approach.

You are one who is in control of your accessing this form of communication. It is not that you are ready at times; it is more that our channels are clearer at one time more than at another. We hope to continue more frequently, but that is not always possible. There is as much interference on this side as there is on "your side!"

We can access the human form through our communication to one who is in body, or we can also choose to be in form. That is what we did while I was on Earth. Our hopes and dreams were conveyed verbally, as well as by our deeds.

Now we can only say that we care what happens as you go about your daily routine. We have no more influence than a "bug on the rug." We are a sounding board or one who listens and speaks what *is*. But we do not intend to influence your decisions. We are just another source of information, all be it a mighty Source that is *All That Is*. But we do not interfere with your life and your decisions. You may continue this work or not. It is up to you.

We only hold the line to the divine Spirit temporarily as you choose this mode of communication. Our work is temporary, too. We have many things to do, many with whom to communicate, for our world is ongoing. It exists, now and forevermore. We engage in our pursuits, just as you do. Our world, here, is Love based, just as yours should be. I say, "Should be" because we often stray from that which we *are*. We recognize ourselves as we progress, but much of the time on Earth we have forgotten our origins. It is Love that permeates our beings, now and forevermore.

So be it.

Later that day

Now is the time to come to the end of our telling of the story of Love. It is for us a tale of Oneness. We cannot help ourselves know more about this well of Love, for it is ever brimming with newness.

Why the end?

It is because we have talked long enough about *Be*-ing Love. One cannot *be* if one is questioning or learning about what *is*. Instead, we come to this point of life knowing about ourselves, about the

Love that lies deep within. We know that we *are* Love. It is our Source of life-giving.

So be it.

And now, we turn to life as a metaphor for everlasting kindness. We are centered *within* ourselves. That does not mean that we are entirely focused upon ourselves and our inner life. Instead it means that we have a promise to keep once we realize who we *are* — it is to spread the Light and the Love to all-else.

We do not shelter our Love and keep it within our own boundries. We radiate both the Love and the Light of our Souls so that others may benefit from our *Be*-ing, here and now. It is a dream that we promise ourselves to share our Light, for we often hide our Love and our Light. To show the world our true Selves is God's greatest gift. To *be* is our message.

No matter where we are, our Light shines so that others may see. Our Love is compassionate so that others may heal their Souls from their own inner *knowing*. We do not pretend to know what is "right" for others. We can only be ourselves, the Selves of our original nature, not those crafted and molded by those around us. Who knows who we really are? Do we?

Up to this point you have kept these writings to yourself. Yes, you have shared them with a few acquaintances but you have hesitated to let people know what you are writing. Can you say that you were truly being yourself when you kept this part of your life hidden? You say that it is only temporary. You wonder what those closest to you will say. What will their reactions be?

To Love is the highest gift one can bestow. To Love is life's only purpose. And yet, you hesitate to share such a loving work. You say that it is because of the way that it came to you that you have been silent. What greater gift is there than the gift of Love?

Raymian

It is sad to see
our tending
to others' business
when
we do not have
our own house
in order. . .

4/29/01 at home

I am sending you a letter of Loving-kindness. That is the epitome of Loving one another. We are One. Therefore, we are of the same Source. We can be unkind in our daily ways. That is, we judge what each other is doing. That is not our business. How one performs is not the root of kindness. Instead, we know that we spur each other onto higher pursuits with encouragement. It is sad to see our tending to others' business when we do not have our own house in order, so to say.

We have much to do to seek that which is our Source. When found, we can encourage all to also find another Source of *Be*-ing within their own lifetime. By that I mean, that we can encourage all to know their Self deeply. It is at that depth that we can operate differently. We *know* who and what we *are*. I cannot tell you what to do. You must make up your own mind.

Our realm is one of Love that is shared throughout *All That Is*. We seek to cover the world with Loving-kindness. By "Loving-kindness" I mean that we are cognizant of each other's foibles, but do not dwell on them. We Love each other to such an extent that each is able to discern his own way. To hold one in Love is to support the growth and knowing of each of us. For those who do not yet recognize who they *are*, we carry hopes of a future filled with one's knowing what is now known.

Raymian

5/4/01 at home

Our words are flowing to the page. We have begun to speak about the spreading of these words. It is bound to happen that you shall spend more time on this project. It will be pleasure to you and to me. And now, I tell you of many other ways of Loving. That is, we can be One, for others are also One.

The man you met on the train is a messenger that you must pay attention to. He said, "Be happy and have no regrets." That is it in a nutshell! Your fellow passenger also said that he likes to look at people and think that they are he, too. That is not quite how it works.

You see others as separate beings. We are connected on another level beyond physical. It is an unseen level of awareness. We know another because we are One with that other, as we are with *all* others. It is as if a stream were flowing through us, picking up our energy where we are and placing it with another. We are still ourselves, and yet we have moved on, here and there at the same time. And we *know* or experience both conditions.

Memory can play a role in this phenomenon. We are just as we have always been, and yet we have had so many experiences that we have been part of. In some ways we are still a part of that long gone experience. The photo shows us in another time and place. We can go to that place in our minds' eyes. We can feel that place and our part in it, yet we are *here* in the here and now.

Weigh the results of our supposition: We *are*, we *have always been*, and we shall *forever be*. That is the promise that is given to us.

So be it.

Raymian

To " know "
is to Be
in the Now
with
the innate knowledge
of
the Self as One.

5/5/01   at home

Now is the time that we know that it is within our Selves that the Light shines. We have hidden the Light under all the Earthly debris collected in this lifetime. Our hearts are open to flow forth with the Light of goodness. By that I mean, we have held back too long our true nature.

It is for us a chore to write words that explain the Light. We need not do this if we were able to convey the beauty of the Light, otherwise. It is almost that we have to resort to words as a primitive form of communication. Do we need words? I don't know. If only we could convey thoughts through the ether in a *knowing*, rather than our *telling* each other.

Thought is powerful in itself. But it, too, is not the only way to access the knowing way of life. When we speak of *knowing*, we are conveying the idea of knowing without thinking, of feeling or trusting another's words or experience. To *know* is to know without learning; it is that you already *know*.

Have you ever looked at the word "know" and seen that the major part of the word is "now?" To *know* is to be in the *now* with the innate knowledge of the Self as One. If *all* is One, then we can access or *know* all there *is* at once.

The state of Oneness allows us to *know* that we are *All That Is*. There is no separateness. I do not "know" anything different from you. We are One; therefore, we *know* each other and ourselves as Oneness.

Our hearts are an entry into the *knowing*. It is the brain that we have relied on in the past. The shift to the heart is Love personified, forevermore.

So be it.

And now, I give you Raymian for a few words about Love inside the human being.

We Love each other throughout the generations. It is not that we go and leave, and come back from birth to death, but that we exist on all levels within the time span. Our hearts are closed at times so that we may experience finding our Source in whatever circumstance. We Love each other, now and forevermore.

We know that life is fleeting. You are experiencing the Light in your heart as it expands. There are many circumstances when we tend to dim that Light as if conserving the fuel source by dampering the fire. It is not necessary to conserve Loving energy. There is an abundance of the Source. We are using that energy to Light the world. It is important that we don't think that there is lack of this Loving energy.

Our hearts tell us that we are coming to a place in the time continuum where we will diverge. It is necessary to see the world in its fullness, not lack. The way to see the world in this newness is to look beyond the point that you have been focusing on. That is, to see beyond the conventionality to a new way of *Be*-ing, open rather than closed, expanding rather than contracting.

Raymian

5/6/01   at home

Today is the first day of deliverance. By that I mean, we have come to a point of knowing that has set us free from not understanding that we know what *is*. It is a freeing feeling that courses through us when we realize that *All That Is, is*. Our hearts are open to this new (for us) way of *Be*-ing: to realize *All That Is* is all there *is*. So be it.

Our hearts are open to "climate control." That is, we can manage our way of *Be*-ing as we do the climate. We create our own inner being or "climate" within. We can be peaceful and calm or we can find within ourselves a stormy climate that is of our own making.

To Love is to hold *within* the peaceful understanding of what Love *is*. It is the purity of the Soul expressing itself as it *is*. We don't allow that *Be*-ing to *be* when we search to fulfill our hopes and dreams by accumulating Earthly wares. It is a sense of knowing that we have within *All That Is*.

Raymian

It is our job
to maintain
our loving nature,
no matter what
the circumstances are.

5/10/01   at home

Our hearts are open to speak with one another. It is a new day for we have passed over the dilemmas of the old way. By that I mean, we have passed into a new way of *Be*-ing. It is sometimes the same as the old way but more often a new way of *Be*-ing. That is, we forget that we have a heart-centered approach, less and less each day. Instead, we remember who we are, a delightful way of being that permeates *All That Is*.

Our hearts are free of old passion for the so-called normal way of life. Instead, we are guided by our inner knowing. It is utmost in our minds and hearts. We know that Love is *All That Is*. It is difficult to say that we *are* Love for there are no words to describe what Love *is*. It *is* what it is.

Now our hearts speak out of Love. They do this by *Be*-ing in the state of Love. We know who is *Be*-ing in this state by melding energies. We are sensing on a higher level what *is* and will *be*.

So be it.

And now, I give you Raymian for a short treatise.

It is for us a long way from where we were on Earth to this place. Our beings have undergone many changes that are noticeable on the surfaces. I am no longer form. You are elderly compared to when we were together. It is change in the dimension that you are experiencing. I am no longer affected by it.

These changes bring their own worries. We think that our hearts might not be as strong as when we were younger, but the *heart of the matter* is as strong today as ever. The heart that I speak of is the inner-dwelling one. It is not the physical heart. It is the center of your being. It is Love personified.

Our hearts are noticeable to us through feelings. We notice a contracted feeling when we are afraid. We notice warmth flowing from us when we are expressing our Loving feelings. It is this Love that we feel, with and from our hearts' Source.

Our hearts dwell within the noblest person that we can conjure. That is, we try to *be* and *express* Love. Other circumstances affect changes in our beings primarily through fearful thoughts. We are and have always been Love. It is our job to maintain our loving nature, no matter what the circumstances are.

And now I give you one more instance of Love being in all that we do. It is our hope that *All That Is* is what you *are*, not what you are *trying* to be. Love is Oneness unsurpassed. *Be* Love. Do not *try* to be, just *be*. Relax and know that *All That Is* is all there is.

Raymian

It sidetracks one
to think that
there is a way
to " accomplish "
a feeling of Lovingness.

We Are Love.

5/13/01 at home

We are *All That Is*. That is all there *is*.

We are enamored with thoughts of Love being something other than what it is. It is what it *is*. We know that we can *be* Love. And yet we fear being *just* Love. We hope that we can be One with *All That Is*, and yet we know not what really *is*. We are confusing our *Be*-ing with reality as it presents itself to us. It is a common way of looking at *what is*.

The looking glass further confuses us for we see ourselves reflected on its surface. Know that what you see is not what *is*. It is a representation of our Earthly bodies. It is not our true essential Self. It is for us to determine what is not on the surface, but below, the hidden way of *seeing*.

We meld our energies with each other. We cannot help from union with each other as we meet on the street. We know that we are of one mind in the greater sense. We Love and are Loved with every passing moment we spend on Earth. We know not that this is so. Instead we feed on hopes of Joy that will come to us at future times. If only we could *do* this or *be* that, then we would *be* Love. That is not the way to recognizing that you are a Loving being. It sidetracks one to think that there is a way to *accomplish* a feeling of Lovingness. We *are* Love. That is acceptable to one who knows that Love is a true way of *Be*-ing.

We conjure up our *Be*-ing — "to be or not to be." We seem confused over what *Be*-ing is. It is a way of knowing that *All That*

Is is what we *are*. We are *All That Is,* in little compartments known as bodies. We are without form when we die, but live in the body for lessons to learn that can be learned only in this way, through the form.

It is not a decision that we take lightly when we decide to incarnate. We know that the way to realizing Love can get rough at times. But it is worth it for our growth and well-being. We know that our hearts' energy will sustain us no matter what we do on Earth. Our hearts are our Source of Loving-kindness. It is true that we are, as we have always been, creatures of Loving-kindness who have chosen to be in this place and in this time. Our hearts are empty when we arrive. Our Souls are *All That Is.* Our moments on Earth are helpful to us in *knowing* forever who and what we *are.*

And now, I bring you Love that is, was and will be, forevermore. Now is the time that we have all waited for: a time that is true Love within and without. We are journeying forward toward a goal when all will realize that Love is within, and Love is *All That Is.*

So be it.

Raymian

Our moments on Earth
are helpful to us
in Knowing
forever
who and what
we Are.

5/16/01   *Chicago O'Hare*

I am looking for a way to be a one who is becoming more than Light. That is, I am seeking a way to find my own inner Light.

Who is speaking?

I am you and you are I. It matters not. Seldom do we communicate with life giving forces that are incarnate. That is, we seldom communicate at this level. Instead we stay away writing on our own hoping someone will be touched by what we have written.

And now, I bring you Raymian, the Light of your life-giving in the moment.

We have much to say to each other. It is not all serious! It is applauded when we work together to make those we know laugh. Can you remember how you would listen intently to all my old jokes, especially the one about D'neice and D'nephew? It was lots of fun fooling and playing with people's humor. I am a born comedian. I loved jokes. The kids at school liked them, too. It was a ritual of passage to tell the same jokes each year to my sixth grade class. They would laugh and laugh, and then tell the same jokes to their friends.

Have you ever noticed how jokes or stories with a punch line are told and appreciated at each age level? It's part of our acculturation process. Everyone who goes through the sixth grade goes through the same jokes. We do not realize sometimes how we structure the education of our young. So is it with every other part of our transmitting of our culture. How else would we learn this trivia?

I remember the day our daughter rode home with me on the train from New York City. She had just come from school in New Jersey where her dorm-mates were playing the new game Trivial Pursuit. Young people pick up the trivia; their parents lived through most of it! So guess who won the game on the train. Our daughter was amazed that her mother knew so much!

Many of us learn by living through circumstances. Others study history and theory. We all know the same thing no matter what our experience is. So it is with the Spirit. We each learn or rediscover in our own way and in our own time. When tested, we are amazed at what we all know. Some of the learning was deliberate. Some of the information was absorbed without even trying. We just knew the answer without having to cram. So it is with our spiritual development. We pick up ideas and knowledge as we go about our daily activities. We process what we experience. That process reveals to us the Truth of what is happening.

Raymian

We each
learn or rediscover
in our own way
and
in our own time.

5/28/01 at home

I am waiting for your call. We have been communicating without writing for the last few days. Ours is a sacred way of knowing. We cannot stop and go without letting each other know what we are about. By that I mean, we care what each other has to say about the ways of life-giving forces. Our hope is to communicate in such a way as to share our experiences.

And now, I bring you Raymian.

So many events have taken place in the last week. It's a wonder that you would think of reaching toward the other side. I, too, saw our grandson play the lead in his third grade school play. He is a magnificent Soul shining forth so that others may see the Love that exudes from him. It will be fun to watch him continue to develop in this lifetime. His role is laid out before him. He shall achieve that which he, too, has agreed to do.

So be it.

Raymian

6/22/01 *flying from Chicago to White Plains*

I am here. I have been watching you as you have moved through life. It is for us a way to know that progression is acceptable at all levels. By that I mean, we can grow to Love ourselves more with each day.

We have known that Love is available from its Source, and yet we do not seek to absorb its Loving ways. Instead we convert our hopes and dreams of a Loving world into one devoid of Love. It is for us to share ways of opening our hearts to the Love that already exists in the inner world. It is to transform our world of Earthly beings into a world of Love that permeates *All That Is*.

It is not to be taken lightly, *knowing* that there is a center of Love within the hearts of *all*. It is to shine forth as an unforgettable way of *Be*-ing. Be not afraid to share what you know with all there is.

Raymian

It is not
to be taken lightly,
Knowing
that there is
a center of Love
within
the hearts of All.

6/24/01 at home 1:00 a.m.

Raymian, What say you?

I *am*, as it is, forevermore. By that I mean, we shall be One *now*, and *forever*. We *are* hearts filled with Love. That is our way of *Be*-ing on Earth. We Love one another forever. We cannot help each other to know the Spirit that lies within. That is accessible only to one who is *All That Is*. We *are* and we *shall be*, forevermore.

I know that you are surprised at our daughters' reactions to your writing. It is for us a way to communicate. For others it is receptiveness that rules the heart. Know that whatever *is* shall always *be*, now and forevermore.

It is important to understand that all that exists, exists for all time. We try to destroy thoughts that we no longer need, but we do not destroy thoughts that exist. We decide that we no longer need to dwell on them or the thought no longer holds any importance to us. It exists, but not for us, as we clear our minds of unwanted thoughts.

The world is filled with Love. That is not just a thought. It is a Loving energy that moves between us, within us and expands beyond us. We generate Loving thoughts. That is the *energy* of Love, plus the *thought* of Love. That is a powerful combination. The thought can conjure up the Love by opening the door to the heart and allowing Love to flow forth. Our Love builds its strength with each passing moment. As we retell our story, others tune into the Love of life that we shared together.

The thought
can conjure up
the Love
by opening the door
to the heart
and allowing
Love to flow forth.

7/1/01   at home

Today is the beginning of one moment that shall be the end of another way of *Be*-ing. By that I mean, we, on this side, are Love beings, not just ones who bring the Light out of darkness. We hover over you in a way that makes us be with you as you go about the daily way of *Be*-ing.

It is not that we are with you in *Be*-ing, but in thoughtfulness. That is, we are always here and you can access our being-ness as you care to. We are always available to do the work that we have committed ourselves to do.

You notice that we have not communicated in writings for awhile. That is because we want to bring about experiences that will enhance the writing. As we live each day, we accumulate experience that is useful to us in understanding better what we are truly about.

Our hearts are open to new ways of *Be*-ing. By that I mean, that we glow in the Light that has been within us for time immemorial. We know that this Light exists for everyone. It glows brighter in those who have an understanding of the Light that is within them. They know, as we know, that Light beams forth with the energy of Love combined with the Light force. It is for us Love and Light together that beams a new way of *Be*-ing in our everyday lives.

We are, therefore, telling a story of Love that combines with Light-ness so that all may see that we are Beings of Light and Love. It has taken us a long time to come to this realization.

Be Love and Light, for that is what you *are*.

So be it.

And now, I bring you Raymian, Soul of life that *is* and shall ever *be*.

Hello! I am glad to see you are again writing to add to our treatise. It has been a long dark month of many experiences which have taken you in many directions that have shown, in their own way, that Love is utmost in our lives.

Our cause is different from our way of being. By that I mean, we know what we are trying to say, and we struggle to compose just the right way of saying it. We need not struggle, for *All That Is* is now and shall ever be. By that I mean, the essence of *All That Is* continues on.

It is true that anything which you create that is material shall not last forever. See the conservation efforts that go into preserving things that are but one hundred years old. These things would not last without that extra effort. So is it with our thoughts and ideas. They do not remain with us unless we give our energies to preserving them in our hearts and minds. Each time that we recall a thought, it gains from that preservation effort. If we don't recall thoughts and experiences, they gradually fade from our reality.

The same goes for thoughts that keep whirling around in our minds. The more that we think those thoughts, the more influence they have on our thoughts of reality. So choose well what you dwell on for that shall be what is real to you.

Raymian

Be
Love and Light,
for that is what
you Are.

7/7/01 at home

Our Love lives on beyond the body. We know that this is true. We also know that Love is everlasting. We cannot know someone so deeply and not recall the Love shared between us. We know that Love is forevermore a way of *Be*-ing, and yet we forget under the delusion of Love making itself known, that we are Love. That is the underlying message of Love-bearing Spirits: that we are Love, nothing else. Our hopes and dreams bear witness to our desire to Love. Our actions show that we do not know that we are already the Love that we seek. We are Love. That is so.

Now that you understand what you are, it is for you to convey the spirit of this message to all you encounter. We cannot be Love and not behold the Love that streams forth from every being. Sometimes we anticipate a loving reaction to something that we have done with kindness. We are disappointed when a grateful loving response is not received in return. We are likewise surprised when we have done nothing and Love is sent our way. Neither of these scenarios is Love as it is meant to be. Instead, Love is a gentleness of spirit that permeates *All That Is*. It is hope fulfilled in a way that nurtures the being.

Love is immortal. It holds neither to convention nor to the body. It moves without intention for it radiates from and permeates *All That Is*. By that I mean, Love is undetectable by ordinary means. It is known to us by our extra-ordinary perception. We *are* Love. We need not *will* Love, for what we *are* permeates *All That Is*.

So be it.

I don't need to have someone tell me that they Love me. I know. It is sensed with the senses of inner knowing. It is felt with the heart of one who knows.

We are all beings, beings who have great ideas and a sense of Loving that are beyond all expectations. We could not imagine the depth and breadth of Love that is our own being. How do we access this illusive sense of our own Selves?

We know that we are beings. What is a being but an accumulation of matter and energy that is mixed with our hopes and dreams? We are an accumulation of our experience, and we are much more. We are the matter, the energy *and* the experiences.

We concentrate on those things that we touch and feel in this three dimensional world. Our senses give us clues to our lives, but those senses also limit our experiences. We cannot convey what we truly *are* through senses that do not access the true Self. We must use other methods to find our loving Self, the Self that is pure Love.

Raymian

Our hopes and dreams
bear witness
to our desire
to Love.

7/11/01   at home

I am that I *am*. We say that many times but do we know what it means? It is for us a way of defining who we are. I am, therefore, I *am*. If I did not know that I existed, would I exist? That is the question that we all have asked. *Am* I? Therefore, I am one who asks; therefore, I *am* or I would not be able to ask!

Our minds dwell on thoughts that have no known way of expression. This is one of those ideas that confounds the questioner. I am, therefore, I *am*, am I not? We look for confirmation of our existence in our way of knowing. We are, therefore, we *are*. One who does not exist cannot make those statements. But what do we mean by existence? Is it as material objects, or is it in a spiritual sense?

At the root of these questions is the root of our existence. Are we body?   Are we mind?   Are we Spirit and something else combined? Or are we only Spirit, putting on a body as we would new clothes, to test out our ways in this Earthly existence?

Our mindful ways teach us that we are more than body. We are that which is sacred. We are wholeness undivided yet individuated. We are at one time both, *All That Is* perfecting ourselves through various experiences on Earth and ourselves as Spirit.

We are learning through Time and space. We are sampling many ways of *Be*-ing in circumstances. At the same time we know that there is but one way to *be* no matter what the circumstance. Our peaceful Loving beings are One with *All That Is,* at every time and in every circumstance.

Raymian

We are
that which is Sacred.

We are wholeness

Undivided

yet

Individuated.

7/14/01   at home

I am, therefore, I *am*.

So be it.

You are wondering why you are out of sorts with yourself. We each go through stages that require us to shed that which is no longer needed. Today is one of those times.

You see that it is likely that you are preparing for a new way to *be* that dwells within the Soul. We are unfolding our destiny. It is not that you are unhappy with circumstance, but that you are dissatisfied with your lot in life. This means that you must seek out the way of life that will be satisfying to the Soul: one that nurtures and adds energy to your circumstances.

You must not dwell in the knowing of the heart that is grieving for lost experiences. Those experiences are always with you. They are never gone completely. You must not dwell in the past of these experiences. You know not why they arise at this time. It is that something has triggered their remembrance, even if you cannot consciously remember the times when these experiences were stored.

Sometimes we forget the details of experience, but the essence remains. It is of this essence that you are letting go. It is because it is the essence that is being released that you cannot conjure up the specific circumstances. We hold the essence of our experiences within our bodies as well as our minds.

We relive the feelings or emotions that we experienced so long ago. We know that these were meaningful to us and left an impression on us. It is time to clear out the residue so that room is made available for new and different experiences. All that we do or experience is impressed upon us. Let go of all that has accumulated so as to move to a higher level of Lightness.

I am forever One with *All That Is*. We are forever One with *All That Is*. Our hearts and minds direct us to new levels of "be." We must unlearn, unwind and remove barriers that keep us from recognizing new levels of *Be*-ing.

Our hearts are open to Loving in new ways. Our hearts are guiding our way. It is a new way of *Be*-ing in the world to be guided by the heart rather than the mind.

So be it.

Our hearts are renewed with Loving energies as we experience Oneness with *All That Is*. We are One. We must recognize that Oneness is a way of *Be*-ing, not just an explanation for the way of the Spirit. It is for us learning again about Love that exists, forevermore.

Our hearts are educated just as our minds were educated. We were told what Love is from a narrow perspective. Indeed Love is most encompassing. It is not narrow or directed. It is all encompassing. We do not create Love for we *are* Love.

Our hearts are open to this new way of *Be*-ing. In preparation, you are letting go of stored energy or memory that is no longer useful and could form a barrier to where you currently want to go.

Go forth in Love and Lightness of Spirit. It is indeed a new way of *Be*-ing.

And now I give you one who wants to share more with you. You are One. He is One with *All That Is*. We are *all* One. So be it.

Raymian

We must unlearn,
unwind and remove
barriers
that keep us
from recognizing
new levels
of Be-ing.

7/15/01 at home

We are One. That is the way of Be-ing that eludes our way of understanding. How can we be One with All That Is and still be ourselves, apparently separate from all others?

It is an illusion that you are separate. What you thought about being separate is also part of this illusion. We must change our focus from one who is *viewing* the world to one who *is* the world.   By that I mean, we are *All That Is*. We are coming from wholeness. Our consciousness is all there is.

We have had a narrow focus that we must shift to the greater good.   By that I mean, we throw ourselves into the midst of the elemental being. That is who we *are*, an aspect of *All That Is*. In *Be*-ing that aspect we take on boundries that seemingly divide us out of the wholeness. We do not lose our *Be*-ing of wholeness. We merely transfer our focus from the *whole* to the *individuated* Soul.

We now must rejoin ourselves to the overall wholeness by shifting our way of *Be*-ing to one that is more universal rather than one focused on individuation. To see oneself as part of the greater whole is to remember that from which we originated. To see ourselves as an aspect of greater *Be*-ing, we remove the barriers of individuation that were necessary in establishing our individual identity.

We are now open to a new experience, one that recognizes who we *are*, fully.   It will influence *how* we are in this world, and beyond. We need not wait to pass over to experience the fullness of *All That Is*.

Raymian

To see oneself
as part
of
the greater Whole
is to remember
that from which
we originated.

7/16/01 at home

So it is that we are here, gathering our thoughts and minds to establish a new way of thinking. It is not that our hearts *think*; it is that our hearts *know*.

How can we differentiate between "thinking" and "knowing?"

The origin of our thought is mind. It helps us to know through our having experiences, not only "hands on," but also through reading and otherwise learning of others' experiences.

The heart, on the other hand, has access to all that there is to know. It is our hearts' voice that is speaking to us now. It is Love that carries the message of a hopeful new way. We are grooming ourselves to expose our way of thinking as summoning up thoughts that explain what we *do* or *know*.

In the West we have been told that we must prove everything. We must not just trust the answer. We may not propose that something is so just because it is so. We must have reasons for what we do. It is not true unless we can *prove* it. It is a slow process to prove our thoughts are right or wrong!

We are now experiencing a renaissance of ideas and ways. It is a melding of what we know from heart and mind together. We cannot prove everything we know. We just *know* that it is so.

So much of what we proved in the past was based on narrow interpretation bounded by the barriers of what we have already proven. What if the basis for all our postulating was not true even though we accepted it at the time? Would we choose new methods to explore other possibilities? That is what I am suggesting, that you accept a different premise on which to base your decision-making.

It is looking at things in a new way. Things don't change; the way we view them can change. Our perspective is open to change. It is no longer blinding us to the potential of other possibilities.

This is a most exciting time on Earth. We are changing our perspective. At the present time, half the people in this country see things one way, and the other half see it differently. We always have a swing or shift in the overall viewpoint. We have an opportunity to choose our direction. Who shall lead the way?

Our ever-changing attitudes need some new perspective, for if we continue in the same ways, we will continue to tread water. The times call out for a deepening of our hearts' Love to be shed on those topics which draw us away from *All That Is*.

We cannot speculate about the future. We can *know* that it is bright.

So be it.

Raymian

Things don't change;
the way
we View them
can change.

7/18/01 at home

Tell me how All That Is being conveyed on these pages is related to our relationship?

It is an example of Loving beyond the world in which you find yourself. You are not only experiencing life on Earth, you are also experiencing a crossing over of the dimensions. That is, you are living in more than one world and place at one time.

Let me explain that further. We are One, that is, we are not separate. We choose to focus on life for the time being. We also have abilities to access other realms. We need no longer shut out the communication from beyond the Earth realm. We are part of a greater Whole. You are merely accessing that greater Whole through this means of communication.

We agreed that you would do this with me at this time before we agreed to a plan for your life experience. Do not get me wrong, we agreed to a *direction*. You had a choice as to whether you engaged in this process at this time.

There are many who believe in and who communicate with Souls no longer incarnate. These letters are to provide an example of one who learns through this process.

We are bound to our purpose: to provide a way of communicating and incorporating that into our everyday lives. We recognize our spiritual side must play a greater part in life on Earth to guide our Souls in our development.

We are agreed that communicating with one who has passed over provides comfort and sustenance. It does not take the place of the things one needs to do on Earth. It is instead a guiding force that can be accessed as needed.

We have spent much time together in the past year creating this document. It is a labor of Love. Our emphasis will change in the future, but for now enjoy the experience and learn from it. Our mission is to open the heart's *knowing* to One's consciousness. We are beings of Love. We grow and nurture through recognizing the Love that dwells within each of us. To know who you truly *are*, you must be aware of loving *within*.

So be it.

We are open to ideas and thoughts surrounded by Love. We share these thoughts and ideas for the betterment of humankind. We Love you and bring you peace and glory that exists within the hearts of all humankind.

Raymian

. . . communicating with
one who has passed over
provides comfort
and sustenance.
It does Not
take the place
of the things
one needs to do
on Earth.

8/15/01   Saratoga Springs, New York

Raymian,

I am wondering if this is the end of the book?

Yes, Denice, we are finished. It has been a delightful journey through the pages. Our Love will be shared so that all will *know* of possibility.

You are Oneness, so am I.

We are *One*, now and forevermore.

Raymian

So be it.

About the Author

Denice Fecketter wrote *Now and Forevermore* in the spare moments between the everyday busy-ness that we all encounter. In the twenty-three years since her husband's death she has been employed as a teacher, extension agent, parliamentarian, executive and a management consultant. She has written non-fiction articles for local, national and international magazines, parented two daughters and traveled extensively. One of her most inspiring trips was to New Zealand to welcome the first dawn of the new millennium, aboard the Tallship Soren Larsen, in the world's first time zone, as shown on the cover.

Acknowledgements

My thanks to those who have helped me in preparing for and supporting me on my journey through in these pages:

Eileen Smith Prokes, my friend and fellow traveler, who is on a similar path and joined me for many meals to share our writings. Knowing someone else whose experiences paralleled mine helped me to know that this communication is not that very far out of the ordinary, but a natural phenomenon that is accessible to all who consider it a possibility.

Dr. Ralph D. Gillespie who was the first to digitize my millennium photo, as well as answer my computer questions.

Annette Chaudet, my editor, publisher and designer who guided the transition from manuscript to book. John Belobraidic for his invaluable computer expertise.

My teachers, who opened my world to unlimited possibilities Dr. Barbara L. Osborn, Dr. James Gauer, Dr. Hedy Milicevic, and Rev. Bill and June Burke.

Members of the Westchester Women's Writers and the International Women's Writing Guild with whom I shared excerpts and received loving advice.

My daughters, who understand that I must go my own way and support me in doing my own thing.

Raymian, Ramon, Armand and Raymond who are co-creators of this book of Love.

Index of Quotes

Our forgiveness is life-giving, both to ourselves and to those who annoy us. 220, 221

Our hearts are filled with Love. It is for us a magnificent gift that explodes the myth that we are evil. 85, 87

Our hearts are formed within the shell of our body on Earth, but there is no limit to their depth or breadth. 148, 149

Our hearts' desire is to find the core of our Selves. It is *within*. 43, 44

Our hearts generate the *knowing*, not the *thinking*. We Know without thought. 159, 160

Our hopes and dreams bear witness to our desire to Love. ..261, 263

Our lives on Earth are temporary forms of who we *are*. 19, 21

Our love did not die when I left. 22, 24

Our Love is the tie that binds our two worlds together. 14, 16

Our love of doing is waning as we tire of constantly *doing* without *renewing*. 223, 227

Our moments on Earth are helpful to us in Knowing forever who and what we Are. 248, 249

Smiles born of Love are catching! 194, 195

That is a way of sages: to know what *Is* without trying to control it in any way. 201, 202

Printed in the United States
1308200002B/226-348